A Guide to Analyzing and Interpreting
ECERS-3
DATA

Richard M. Clifford • Noreen Yazejian
Wonkyung Jang • Dari Jigjidsuren

FOREWORD BY DEBI MATHIAS

TEACHERS COLLEGE PRESS

TEACHERS COLLEGE | COLUMBIA UNIVERSITY
NEW YORK AND LONDON

Published by Teachers College Press,® 1234 Amsterdam Avenue, New York, NY 10027

Library of Congress Cataloging-in-Publication Data

Names: Clifford, Richard M., author. | Yazejian, Noreen M., author. |
    Jang, Wonkyung, author. | Jigjidsuren, Dari, author.
Title: A guide to analyzing and interpreting ECERS-3 data / Richard M. Clifford,
    Noreen Yazejian, Wonkyung Jang, Dari Jigjidsuren.
Other titles: Guide to analyzing and interpreting Early Childhood Environment
    Rating Scale 3 data
Description: New York : Teachers College Press, [2021] | Includes bibliographical
    references and index.
Identifiers: LCCN 2021030144 (print) | LCCN 2021030145 (ebook) |
    ISBN 9780807766071 (Paperback : acid-free paper) | ISBN 9780807766088
    (Hardcover : acid-free paper) | ISBN 9780807779934 (eBook)
Subjects: LCSH: Classroom environment—United States—Evaluation. |
    Early childhood education—United States—Evaluation. | Day care centers—
    United States—Evaluation. | Play schools—United States—Evaluation.
Classification: LCC LB3011.5 .C55 2021 (print) | LCC LB3011.5 (ebook) |
    DDC 372.210973—dc23
LC record available at https://lccn.loc.gov/2021030144
LC ebook record available at https://lccn.loc.gov/2021030145

ISBN 978-0-8077-6607-1 (paper)
ISBN 978-0-8077-6608-8 (hardcover)
ISBN 978-0-8077-7993-4 (ebook)

Printed on acid-free paper
Manufactured in the United States of America

Contents

Foreword

I have had the good fortune of witnessing the evolution and impact of the Environment Rating Scale (ERS) tools throughout my career. In the 1980s, as the administrator of a small child care center in Pennsylvania, I oversaw its growth into a multisite operation incorporating children funded by Head Start, child care subsidies, and private-pay families. As the quality of the early learning environment became more of a focal point, our team began exploring possible tools to help improve the teaching and learning experiences for children. We settled on the ERS tools because we felt they could give us a more explicit understanding of the research-based elements necessary to create the conditions for success and serve as a protocol for orienting new teachers in our approach. They gave the teachers specific ideas about changes they could make to improve their practices to better serve children as they dug deeper into understanding how and why the scale items were related to quality settings.

In 2005, as the first director of early learning in Pennsylvania, I focused on development, implementation, and scaling of the Keystone STARS quality improvement program. The team and advisory committee selected the ERS tools as part of the framework for the quality improvement system for a variety of reasons: the coverage it provided for different settings and age groups (infant/toddler, preschool, school-age programs, and home-based settings); the opportunity it offered for consistent application across the state; its reliability as a research-based accountability metric on how the system was working for funders and other stakeholders; and its ability to guide program and provider efforts. The data the tools provided informed technical assistance efforts and providers as they prioritized quality improvement efforts. A bonus was the close relationship and open communication we had with the authors, who continually asked for our input as they sought a deeper understanding of how the tools were working in the field.

As the authors focused on improving the tools so that they would measure global quality from the perspective of the child, they were guided by current literature review, analysis of extant ECERS-R data, consideration of practitioner feedback, and results of the ECERS-3 pilot. Now the authors offer *A Guide to Analyzing and Interpreting ECERS-3 Data*, a treasure trove of information for those who want a deeper understanding of their conceptual models, of the influences impacting their framework of examining quality as global construct, of the deep research and statistical analysis of the tool, and of the connection between research and practice.

There is something for everyone in this book. Directors, practitioners, and providers will find informative both the educational theory behind the tools and how the authors have used data and analysis to update the tools. Technical assistance providers, coaches, and program staff will discover how the data can inform continuous quality improvement efforts and advance reflective practice. State leaders will find a solid research base and research-to-practice examples as a reference for policy decisions. Through the data, they will better understand the quality of the programs in their state and how supports are working to help providers improve their quality. This analysis of the ECERS-3 is generalizable to the ITERS-3 and FCCERS-3. Researchers will find the data, interpretations, and statistical methods—especially those applied from other disciplines—fascinating.

And there's so much more of interest:

- the authors' examinations of factors, including length of day; teacher/child ratio; age differences; proportion of children who are Black, Hispanic, and have disabilities; lead teacher and director education and experience; and wages that could influence policy
- the association of the ECERS-3 score with executive function
- the descriptions of quality as reflected in the ECERS-3 for different program types, such as child care, Head Start, and state pre-K, and how this relates to quality standards above licensing for programs not following the Head Start or pre-K standards
- the authors' descriptions of "quality for a day" versus the creation of ongoing sustainable improvements in quality
- how the diversity of children and staff has been addressed through changes in specific indicators throughout the scale

to increase sensitivity to the full range of needs of children, regardless of race, ethnicity, gender identity, country of origin, or ability

The tools have been translated into multiple languages and used internationally. It is particularly encouraging to read the authors' reflections on next steps for the tool and that additional studies of the ECERS-3 are needed to understand possible differences in experiences of quality among different racial groups and classrooms with different racial mixes. The authors also plan to examine the racial-ethnic match between children and staff, as well as between staff and the ECERS observer. The esteemed authors—Richard M. Clifford, Noreen Yazejian, Wonkyung Jang, and Dari Jigjidsuren—bring a rigorous research background, excellent academic credentials, and years of experience in measuring global quality in early learning settings to their work.

We owe our appreciation to the authors for moving forward the critical conversation on high-quality learning environments.

—Debi Mathias,
Director, ECE Quality Improvement Systems, BUILD Initiative

Acknowledgments

We are grateful to the vast number of colleagues who have contributed to the development of the ECERS. Experts and practitioners have provided us with great insight into how early childhood environments affect young children's development across all developmental domains. This information has shaped the way we constructed this assessment instrument. It is impossible to mention every individual who has contributed to this work, but we do want to acknowledge those who played a significant role in the development of this guide:

- Special thanks are due to the other authors of the ECERS-3. Our long-term author colleagues, Thelma Harms and Debby Cryer, have helped in so many ways with this guide. Their seminal work in studying early learning environments is central to the development of this book.
- Other colleagues at the Environment Rating Scales Institute, especially Cathy Riley and Tracy Link.
- Many researchers at Frank Porter Graham Child Development Institute at the University of North Carolina at Chapel Hill who have used the ECERS in studies and given us their feedback on strengths and weaknesses of the instrument in its different editions. In particular, we would like to thank John Sideris (now at the University of Southern California) for his groundbreaking work on using Item Response Theory methods in examining the properties of the ECERS. Diane Early (now at Child Trends), Jen Neitzel (now at the Educational Equity Institute), Kelly Maxwell (now at Child Trends), and Ellen Peisner-Feinberg (now at the UNC School of Education) have all been generous in their support and help as we have made modifications to the ECERS over many years and influenced our thinking about the use of the Scales.

- Other research organizations and state agencies who shared the data, with special thanks to leaders in North Carolina, Georgia, Pennsylvania, Washington, Arkansas, and Louisiana.
- Mark Branagh and his colleagues at the Branagh Information Group for their ongoing support with obtaining and managing data as well as their overall support for all things ERS.
- Agencies and individuals who volunteered their time and effort.
- Professor Kathy Sylva, Oxford University, UK, and the ECERS International Working Group.
- Translators who have produced official editions of the ECERS in more than 20 languages, as well as dozens of research editions used for specific studies around the world.
- Editors and other colleagues at Teachers College Press, Columbia University.
- Teachers and administrators who have welcomed us to their programs to test out new ideas for the ECERS and to provide advice on its use in their settings.

CHAPTER 1

Introduction

The Early Childhood Environment Rating Scale (ECERS)* is one in a family of Environment Rating Scales (ERS) that uses in-person observation to assess the quality of children's early care and education settings. The first version of the ECERS was published in 1980 (Harms & Clifford), with major revisions published in 1998 (ECERS-R; Harms et al.), and again in 2015 (ECERS-3; Harms et al.). The instrument is designed specifically for classrooms of preschool children from 36 months through 5 years of age in center-based care and education settings. The ECERS-3 assesses the physical environment, children's interactions with one another and with significant adults, activities within cognitive and social domains, as well as children's health and safety, to provide an overall measure of classroom environment quality. Early childhood is a crucial stage in a child's life, and aspects of the environment in the physical, social-emotional, cognitive, and health and safety domains all play important roles in shaping children's development during these early years. The physical environment, child's relationships, and instruction are all intertwined in support of young children's development. Having a valid and reliable measure of the quality of these aspects of children's care settings is critical. The ECERS has become the most widely used early childhood environment quality assessment tool in both the United States and the world. This assessment has been used in more than 20 countries and has been formally published in more than 20 languages.

---

* The authors use "ECERS-3" to refer to the newest, 3rd edition, of the Early Childhood Environment Rating Scale, "ECERS" to refer to the full set of editions of the Early Childhood Environment Rating Scale, and "ERS" to refer to the full family of Environment Rating Scales, including the ECERS, ITERS (Infant–Toddler Environment Rating Scale), and FCCERS (Family Child Care Environment Rating Scale) in their various editions.

PURPOSE OF THE GUIDE

The intent of this guide is to provide extended descriptive information on the ECERS-3, including psychometric properties of the measure. Using a large-scale data set of ECERS-3 observations, the guide examines how ECERS-3 scores relate to each other, within and across Subscales, and within the scale as a whole, including whether other structures besides the Subscales might provide further insight into the underlying concept of quality. The guide describes how scores on the previous version, ECERS-R, relate to scores on the ECERS-3. While this large sample is not representative of the full population of early childhood classrooms in the United States, information on the distribution of scores at Item, Subscale, and total score levels for the full combined data set is provided. This set of facts and figures is provided to give a general idea of how programs score in order to help users interpret their own findings from using the ECERS-3, but it should not be used to judge the level of quality in the United States.

The information provided here also shows ECERS-3 scores by characteristics of the classroom settings, including education level of lead teachers, ages of children served, the presence of one or more children with a disability, and the number of children enrolled. This guide builds on the psychometric data gathered as part of the pilot and field tests of the ECERS-3 and presented in the ECERS-3 itself. In addition, extensive examples of ways of portraying data from ECERS-3 are shown. It is hoped that the information contained herein will be useful to program directors, agency administrators, researchers, and others who use the ECERS-3 for documenting quality, guiding quality improvement, and examining associations between quality and children's outcomes. A chapter on special issues in using the ECERS-3 discusses points that have been raised in use of the Scales in the United States and other countries.

EARLY CHILDHOOD LEARNING ENVIRONMENTS: A CONCEPTUAL FRAMEWORK

This section begins with a description of early childhood in the context of life in our world. We begin with a brief overview and then proceed with a framework for thinking about how children learn and develop, a theory of change, and finally a conceptual framework of early learning environments and their impact on young children.

The past century has witnessed profound changes in family organization, work life, and the emergence of early childhood education and care as a significant feature of the lives of young children and their families in the period leading up to entrance into the formal education system. These changes are interrelated. The role of women in the paid labor force has affected not only women themselves but also the lives of their families. In the United States, women were called to enter the paid workforce during World War II after large proportions of men joined the armed services and were no longer available to participate in the economy (Goldin, 1991). This shift led to the creation of a network of federally supported early childhood services, including child care centers, to support the families experiencing these changes. After the war, many men returned to their old jobs, replacing the women who had stepped in to take their places, thus returning large numbers of women to traditional family care responsibilities. The supportive services mostly disappeared. But the experience demonstrated that women were fully capable of participation in the paid labor force and changed expectations for both women and men profoundly. Gradually, more women found that work outside the home was a good fit for them because it provided personal and financial advantages for them and their families. Changes may have seemed slow at the time, but by historic standards developments in family life and structure have been quite rapid. In 1950, most children were reared at home with their mothers. By 1980, most preschool-aged children were in child care or other nonparental learning settings (Snyder et al., 2018). Furthermore, by 2000, approximately 60% of all women of working age were in the paid labor force. By comparison, during the Industrial Revolution men moved from working at home, mainly in farming, to working away from home. It took 200 years to see a level of impact on men's work comparable to the changes for women in the second half of the last century (Kammerman & Gatenio, 2003).

These changes have been felt around the world. The Organisation for Economic Co-operation and Development (OECD) has conducted studies of various countries' early childhood services and finds a large expansion of services across the 37 OECD member countries (OECD, 2017). OECD member countries are primarily economically advanced, but the World Bank and other international organizations have supported improvement and expansion of ECE in less-developed countries (World Bank, 2019; WHO, 2016).

This very brief discussion is not intended to be a comprehensive look at forces affecting early childhood services; however, it does illustrate the impact of changes in the larger environment on young children in our world. Our societies still struggle with how social and political institutions can and should react to these changes in family life—and young children are perhaps most affected by this process.

VIEWS OF HOW CHILDREN LEARN AND DEVELOP

Urie Bronfenbrenner, in his classic book *The Ecology of Human Development* (1979), presents a model for understanding the influences affecting children's development (see Figure 1.1). His ecological systems theory suggests that there is a network of factors in children's lives that range from distal factors, such as cultural norms and ideology, laws, and customs (referred to as the Macrosystem), to gradually more proximal factors. The larger social system does not directly affect the child, but does affect them indirectly through the more proximal

Figure 1.1. Bronfenbrenner's Bio-Ecological Systems Theory

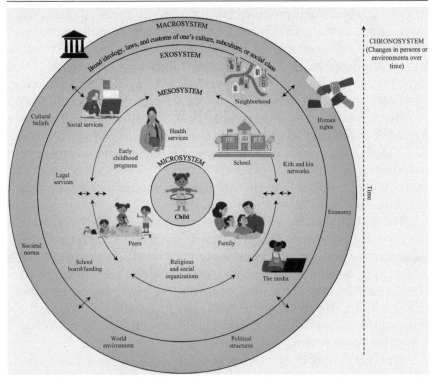

elements in one's community, such as businesses and industry, extended family and neighbors, the media, and the legal system. These elements, referred to as being in the Exosystem, in turn affect the Mesosystem, including family, school, and religious and social institutions, among others. Early learning environments are located within the Mesosystem. All of these elements have a powerful impact on children. It should be noted here that the effects also travel in the opposite direction. For instance, changes in a child's health affect the family and in turn the other more distal features of this model. The ECERS is designed to examine the influences of the early childhood learning environment on children as they learn and develop. Bronfenbrenner also recognized that things change over time and that this change must be acknowledged as well. In addition, he understood that there are biological features within children that affect development. This theory is complex but provides a framework for thinking about how early childhood care and learning environments fit into the much larger picture of influences on children's development.

Other theorists and researchers have debated the influences of nature and nurture. Nature includes the genetic makeup of children, their temperament, and personality, with emphasis on the biological basis of child development. This line of thinking led to the ages and stages of development that are determined by the individual child's constitution (e.g., Gesell maturational theory [Gesell & Ilg, 1943]; Crain, 2000). On the other hand, nurture emphasizes the interactive processes of the child and environment more in line with Bronfenbrenner's point of view. Current conceptualizations espouse a dynamic interaction between nature and nurture, and the need for investigations that combine genetic, environmental, and developmental research frameworks and methods to understand child development (Rutter, 2002). Overall, children's development is a combination of these two aspects of development. The primary focus in the creation of the Environment Rating Scales is on the nurture side of child development.

The thinking of Bronfenbrenner led the authors to consider the full environment of early childhood programs because each element affects the child, often in conjunction with other elements of the program. The construction of the ECERS recognized the interconnectedness of factors that impact children in early childhood environments. It also recognizes that all aspects of children's development—physical, cognitive, and social-emotional, as well as their health and safety—are interconnected. Development in each of these domains influences development in the others.

In considering how children learn, Lev Vygotsky (1978) recognized the social nature of learning, and specifically the importance and nature of interactions that influence learning. Fundamental to learning is Vygotsky's identification of the concept of the reciprocal nature of interactions as the heart of children's learning across areas of development. Specifically, the adult's understanding of where the child is developmentally, and then the adult challenging and supporting the child to move a little out of their comfort zone—what he referred to as the "zone of proximal development"—is what drives the learning process.

Executive function, the set of thinking skills that include working memory, flexible thinking, and self-control, is especially important for success in school and later life and deserves particular mention. These skills have been linked to early academic skills in literacy and math domains (Schmitt et al., 2017). In addition, children with higher executive functioning demonstrate better social-emotional skills (Burchinal et al., 2020). Evidence suggests that global classroom quality as measured with the ECERS-3 is associated with executive function (Early et al., 2018). It has been argued that the specific content of the ECERS-3, namely Items in the Learning Activities and Interactions Subscales, map onto executive function, given the emphases in the Items in those Subscales on children making decisions within open-ended activity settings guided by teacher scaffolding, as well as opportunities for peer interaction (Early et al., 2018).

THEORY OF CHANGE

The theory of change presented here seeks to combine understanding of how children learn and develop with how early education and care fit into the process of improving the path to development for children, and eventually the long-term outcomes for children in our society. First, as shown in Figure 1.2, many factors external to early learning environments contribute to children's development. These factors are similar to what Bronfenbrenner includes under Macrosystems, and some that he categorizes as part of the Mesosystem. This theory of change places the direct experiences of children in early childhood settings in a box that is sometimes referred to as the "black box." This term is meant to indicate that it is not clear what the full range of experiences are for children in these settings and how those experiences of children are related to the impact on their development. The

Figure 1.2. Theory of Change

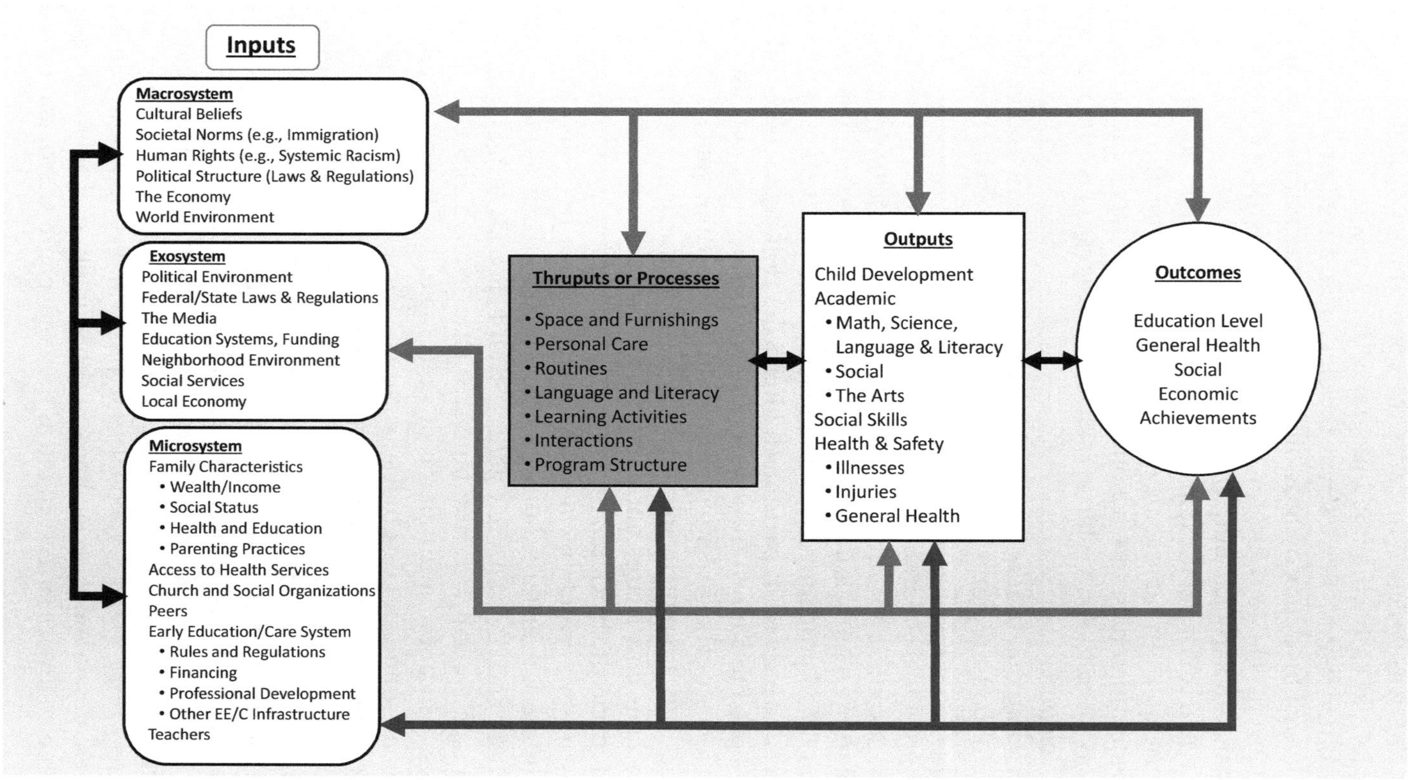

Inputs

Macrosystem
Cultural Beliefs
Societal Norms (e.g., Immigration)
Human Rights (e.g., Systemic Racism)
Political Structure (Laws & Regulations)
The Economy
World Environment

Exosystem
Political Environment
Federal/State Laws & Regulations
The Media
Education Systems, Funding
Neighborhood Environment
Social Services
Local Economy

Microsystem
Family Characteristics
• Wealth/Income
• Social Status
• Health and Education
• Parenting Practices
Access to Health Services
Church and Social Organizations
Peers
Early Education/Care System
• Rules and Regulations
• Financing
• Professional Development
• Other EE/C Infrastructure
Teachers

Thruputs or Processes
• Space and Furnishings
• Personal Care
• Routines
• Language and Literacy
• Learning Activities
• Interactions
• Program Structure

Outputs
Child Development
Academic
• Math, Science, Language & Literacy
• Social
• The Arts
Social Skills
Health & Safety
• Illnesses
• Injuries
• General Health

Outcomes
Education Level
General Health
Social
Economic
Achievements

ECERS was designed to clarify the opportunities available to children in formal early childhood programs that support their development. In other words, ECERS was developed as an effort to define what is in that black box by providing a working definition of what leads to change in children in preschool classrooms—what we refer to as the quality of early learning environments.

To understand the impact of quality on children's development, one must look at what is going on inside the classroom. How do various activities, materials, interactions, use of time, and learning opportunities work to influence children's skills and abilities across the full range of development?

Note that factors outside the formal learning environment in early childhood programs also influence children's development through other avenues. For example, parent income can influence the nature of programs children enter and the quality of learning environments, but income also affects other learning and enrichment experiences (learning materials in the home, travel, special classes outside the early childhood program, etc.). Those factors outside the box have both direct and indirect impacts on children's development. The ECERS is not designed to address those external factors. Included in those external factors are what are often referred to as structural quality. The ECERS does not attempt to measure those structural inputs. Figure 1.2 illustrates how factors outside the black box, "inputs," affect what goes on inside the black box (quality of early learning settings) and subsequently the children's developmental change (outputs) and eventually the longer-term outcomes for children, such as success later in school and life and their general well-being. To bring about positive change we can alter the inputs, such as state and local public policies, education and training of staff, materials, financial support for the program, and external supervision. These include those structural elements of quality mentioned above. These influences outside the box may directly influence children's development through some avenue outside the early childhood program, as well as affect the quality of the early childhood program. Structural elements are primary ways to impact the processes in the black box (quality).

As shown in Figure 1.2, the quality of early childhood programs impacts children's knowledge, skills, and abilities, as well as their health, safety, and social-emotional and physical development. Ultimately, these newfound skills, abilities, health, and physical abilities help determine children's success in life as they move into school and eventually adulthood and the larger world—these are the outcomes we hear so much about. So, life is truly complex.

The Early Childhood Environment Rating Scales focus on one small but important aspect of this complexity—early childhood learning environments for young children—in a way that recognizes that complexity but also clarifies thinking into making these early childhood environments a happier, healthier, and more stimulating place for children.

ASSESSING QUALITY

So, what is this element referred to as "quality" in early childhood settings?

Quality in early childhood classrooms can be measured and viewed from a variety of perspectives. What do parents most want? What do preschool teachers want? How about administrators? Or kindergarten teachers? Then there are researchers, policymakers, and politicians. From the very beginning of our work in the mid-1970s, the authors chose to look at learning environments from the perspective of the children who are spending a substantial proportion of their lives—more than 50% of their waking time for some—in these environments. From the perspective of a child, important questions about quality include the following:

1. Is this a safe place for me?
2. Am I getting a healthy and nourishing experience?
3. Is the environment stimulating for me both cognitively and physically?
4. Do I have opportunities to develop healthy relationships with other children and with adults?
5. Am I being provided enough guidance and freedom to help me become an independent and self-sufficient individual? (Clifford et al., 2020).

Quality as conceived by the authors is a measure of how well early childhood environments meet these needs of children in early childhood settings across the full range of development. As described above, millions of factors—interactions with staff and other children, materials and supplies and their use with children, the use of time, transitions, and routine care activities, to name just a few—impact children in preschools, child care centers, schools, and other group-based learning settings. The ERS instruments, including ECERS-3, measure only a small part of the broad array of features that affect children in these settings. The Scales examine a sample of these factors that influence children's development as a means of measuring quality.

The ECERS-3 consists of 461 indicators scored *yes* or *no*. Seventeen indicators may be scored *NA* under defined circumstances. Item scores are determined by the indicator scores and assigned a score of 1 to 7. Two Items may be scored *NA* under specifically described circumstances. The 35 Items are grouped into a set of six Subscales. Subscale scores are calculated as the mean of the Item scores in each Subscale. These Subscales are based on the organization and operation of early childhood settings to facilitate data collection. It is recommended that the Subscale scores be interpreted carefully, since they have not been confirmed previously using factor analytic approaches. Researchers have combined Items in other ways based on factor analyses or item response theory methods (see Cassidy et al., 2005, for ECERS-R factors; Early et al., 2018, for ECERS-3 factors; Sideris et al., 2014, for Item Response Methods for identifying new "virtual Subscales" based on indicator scores for ECERS-R). These are described in more detail in subsequent chapters.

The total score is calculated as the mean of all Item scores (excluding any Items marked as *NA*). This total quality score is considered the best estimate of the overall, global quality of a classroom or program, and is based on the overall 461 indicators of quality. This global quality score is seen as more than a simple sum of all the aspects scored in the indicators. It is the best estimate of the full range of factors in the environment that affect children's development. It is impossible to measure all the elements in these environments. It is only possible to measure a small sample of the millions of elements to estimate the full quality of early learning settings. However, this overall concept of quality can be broken down into distinct aspects of the environment—thus there are separate Item and Subscale scores.

Many instruments have been designed to measure various aspects of quality (e.g., Caregiver Interaction Scale [Arnett, 1989], the Classroom Assessment Scoring System—Pre-K [CLASS Pre-K; Pianta et al., 2008], and the Early Literacy and Language Classroom Observation [ELLCO; Smith et al., 2002]), but the ECERS is the only major instrument that attempts to examine the full range of factors in the environment that affect the totality of children's development.

CHAPTER 2

ECERS-3 Background

Development of the ECERS began in the 1970s. The scale has undergone regular revisions as new information has emerged and the early childhood field's measurement needs have evolved. This chapter provides background information on the ECERS and a description of the Subscales and Items that comprise the ECERS-3.

EARLY WORK IN ASSESSING LEARNING ENVIRONMENTS

In 1976, Thelma Harms and Richard Clifford began development of an instrument designed to assess the quality of early learning environments. This work grew out of a project at the Frank Porter Graham Child Development Center (FPG) at the University of North Carolina at Chapel Hill to provide in-service education and training to county day care coordinators in local North Carolina departments of social services. Clifford led this project and asked Harms to conduct a seminar session for the group focusing on improving learning environments. At the time, Harms was the director of Early Childhood Education Curriculum Development at FPG. The training session was a tremendous success, and participants asked for a document that could help them as they returned to their own counties to work with day care center personnel. Harms and Lee Cross, the director of the child care center at FPG at the time, developed a document for the group entitled *Environmental Provisions in Day Care*, which included a checklist of items to consider when working with day care centers. Based on this work, Harms and Clifford eventually created a more formal instrument that could be used to assess the quality of the provision of day care and that could be used reliably by observers.

The Day Care Environment Rating Scale (Harms & Clifford, 1978) was printed in large enough quantities to allow for data collection to assess the psychometric properties of this new instrument. During the next 2 years, a small series of tests of the Scale confirmed that the instrument could be used reliably by trained observers to provide consistent and meaningful results. The Scale consisted of 38 Items conceptually organized into seven Subscales:

- Personal Care of Children
- Furnishings and Display for Children
- Language and Reasoning Experiences
- Fine and Gross Motor Activities
- Creative Activities
- Social Development
- Adult Needs

The Scale was designed to be used across all age groups in day care centers, from infants to preschoolers. Of the 38 Items, 10 were omitted when scoring rooms with only infants enrolled, and an additional 5 Items had alternate Items for infant groups. Each Item was scored using a 4-point Likert-type scale with anchor descriptions for each of the 4 points.

By late 1979, additional edits to the Day Care Environment Rating Scale were made based on the 2 years of its use. Teachers College Press published the newly revised version, the Early Childhood Environment Rating Scale (ECERS), in 1980. The original ECERS contained 37 Items organized into seven Subscales. In this version, each Item was presented as a 7-point Likert-type scale with four descriptions representing quality levels at 1, 3, 5, and 7 on the scale. When scoring the scale, both observation and interview techniques were used—interviews could be of the director and/or the teacher(s). Assessors were instructed to start at the lowest end of the quality scale and read the descriptions; if a classroom met the requirements of the description, the assessor went to the next quality-level description. Scores between the four levels— at 2, 4, and 6—were assigned when aspects of the quality descriptions were determined by the assessor to have been partially met.

Beginning in the late 1980s, the ERS was expanded to include two additional versions. In 1989, a new Scale specifically for assessing quality in Family Child Care Homes, the Family Day Care Environment Rating Scale (FDCRS; Harms & Clifford, 1989), was published. At this point, Debby Cryer joined the author group and together with Harms and Clifford produced the Infant/Toddler Environment Rating Scale (ITERS; Harms et al., 1990). These new versions of the Scale maintained the basic structure of the ECERS with the same seven Subscales, but with the content focusing on these two different types of settings.

ECERS REVISIONS PROCESS

In 1996–1998, the authors completed a comprehensive update of the ECERS (ECERS-R; Harms et al., 1998). Following her work with the ITERS, Cryer also served as an author of the new ECERS-R. The ECERS-R consisted of 43 Items organized into the same original seven Subscales, and both observation and interview were still used for scoring. With the ECERS-R, numbered Indicators were provided for each Item at levels 1, 3, 5, and 7. Assessors scored each Indicator as Yes or No depending on whether the classroom met the requirements of the indicator, and specific scoring rules were applied to determine the score on the 1–7 scale based on the indicator responses. As a result of adding indicators, assessors were provided more objective guidance for assigning quality scores to early childhood classrooms. Assessors typically discontinued scoring indicators when an Item had sufficient information to be scored. An updated version of ECERS-R was made available in 2005, retaining the ECERS-R Items and Subscales from the previous edition and providing additional guidance on scoring many of the Items, but without editing the Items themselves (Harms et al., 2005).

In the most recent version of the ECERS, the ECERS-3 (Harms et al., 2015), the use of Indicators scored as yes or no as the basis of determining the 1–7 Item score has remained the same. However, the procedures for the ECERS-3 include the strong recommendation that all Indicators be scored on the assessment, rather than discontinuing Indicator scoring when an Item score is reached; this procedure provides a more complete assessment of the environment and offers better guidance for quality improvement. The ECERS-3 has 35 Items and includes six of the original seven Subscales; the Parent and Staff Subscale was removed because of limited variability in scores and the total reliance on teacher reporting for scoring the Items in that Subscale. While a few questions are asked of the program director to determine numbers of children served and presence of children with disabilities, the ECERS-3 scoring relies fully on observation, rather than on a combination of observation and interview. The observation period was set to exactly 3 hours to standardize observation procedures. In previous editions, the observation time was not clearly defined.

In 2014–2015, revisions to create the new ECERS-3 included substantial changes to the Indicators and the Items in order to improve validity and reliability and reflect the current state of the early childhood field. These changes were guided by four primary sources of information:

1. review of current literature,
2. analyses of extant ECERS-R data,
3. consideration of practitioner feedback, and
4. examination of pilot and field test results for an initial draft of the ECERS-3 measure.

The ECERS authors started by considering the current literature on child development, early childhood curriculum and instruction, health and safety, and emergent classroom challenges, such as use of technology. The literature review led to several changes. For example, additional Items related to language and literacy and to math were added in response to literature highlighting the importance of these domains for young children's development and learning. Guided by literature related to teacher–child interactions, the authors also revised Indicators across the various activity areas of the scale to focus less on children's access to materials and more on how the teachers and children use and interact around the materials. Finally, health and safety Items were modified to reflect current standards.

The revision process was also guided by data, particularly analyses of a large sample of classrooms assessed with ECERS-R across several studies conducted by researchers at the Frank Porter Graham Child Development Institute. Using this large extant data set, which included classrooms that varied along the full continuum of quality but that were slightly less representative of excellent-quality care, the ECERS authors were able to examine how Indicators were functioning within Items and how each Item was functioning in relation to others. In particular, the ECERS authors analyzed Indicator difficulty, or the proportion of no scores to yes plus no scores on each Indicator difficulty=number of no scores/(number of yes+number of no scores),* to ensure that

---

* In calculating the difficulty index, the indicators in the Inadequate column were reverse-scored to match the positive statements in the other three columns.

Indicators were appropriately placed within the 1–7 quality levels of each Item. New Indicators were also written to represent the full scale of quality from 1 to 7 for each Item when the analyses indicated missing information at a particular quality level.

The ECERS authors have always maintained close relationships and open communication with the practitioners—teachers, directors, licensing agency staff, technical assistants, coaches, college faculty, other trainers, and researchers both in the United States and internationally—who represent the end-users of the scale. Along with exchanges with collaborators at the Environment Rating Scales Institute, Inc. (ERSI), who provide training and reliability certification for users of the ECERS, interactions with practitioners and researchers, particularly their questions about the scale, provided another source of information for revisions. The authors' experiences observing in programs, training observers, conducting research in classrooms, and collaborating with designers and implementers of quality rating and improvement systems (QRIS) informed the revisions to the ECERS-3.

Finally, in 2013–2014, the authors conducted a small pilot test and then two larger field tests of the first drafts of the revised scale. The small pilot resulted in minor revisions to clarify wordings of Indicators and the Notes for Clarification. A larger field test was then conducted with trained observers. The results indicated that further refinements were needed. Seven Indicators with low reliability were eliminated, several other Indicators were revised, and the Notes for Clarification for some Items were rewritten to improve clarity and reliability of the Items. A second field test on the resulting revised scale was conducted. The results of this test showed acceptable levels of reliability, and the scale was considered final.

The overall goal in the revision process was to arrive at a scale that was more reliable and valid in its assessment of quality. It was a particular goal to improve the association between quality scores on the scale and children's developmental outcomes. The ECERS authors have constantly strived to improve the scale within the framework of examining quality as a global construct (including multiple domains of the environment) from the perspective of the children in the classroom. The revisions that resulted in the ECERS-3 moved the scale forward, but the authors anticipate that as additional information about child development within the context of center-based child care is learned, further revisions will be needed to improve the scale.

ADMINISTRATION

The ECERS-3 scale includes full details on how to administer the assessment (see ECERS-3, pp. 7–12). That description includes details about the length of time required (3-hour block) and instructions for how to observe the environment, what resources to consult for health and safety requirements, how Items are scored, how Subscales and the total scale scores are calculated, and the use of a classroom profile sheet for summarizing the data. Of note, the total mean score is the sum of all Item scores for the entire scale divided by the number of Items scored, *not* the average of the Subscale scores—the authors have found this to be a common error in practice.

The most important skills for completing the scale are observation, listening, and reading. The first two likely seem obvious—one must be skilled in watching children and staff in the classroom and listening to their interactions and language to determine whether Indicators are met and how to score. The third skill—reading—is just as critical. Observers must carefully *read* the entire scale—each Indicator and the Notes for Clarification—in order to accurately score the Items.

Observing classroom environments is a complex endeavor; while the scoring of the ECERS-3 is determined by patterns of yes and no responses, the scale is much more complicated than a checklist of quality. The Notes for Clarification are a necessary component of the scale to help assessors make accurate determinations about whether the quality Indicators are met. The Notes for Clarification provide descriptions regarding what should be considered, supplementary definitions and examples, and guidance about interpretation for those Indicators that require additional explanation. In brief, these Notes aid in accurately and reliably scoring quality. Occasionally, Notes for Clarification are added to Items when feedback from practitioners or researchers suggests that an Indicator is unclear; these additional notes are maintained on the ERSI website (www.ersi.info), with new updates clearly marked.

OVERVIEW OF THE SUBSCALES

As noted previously, the ECERS-3 consists of 35 Items conceptually organized into six Subscales. Within each Item there are Indicators at quality levels 1, 3, 5, and 7 that are scored as Yes or No to arrive at a score for the Item. Figure 2.1 lists each Item within its Subscale. While

Figure 2.1. ECERS-3 Subscales and Items

SPACE AND FURNISHINGS

1. Indoor space
2. Furnishings for care, play, and learning
3. Room arrangement for play and learning
4. Space for privacy
5. Child-related display
6. Space for gross motor play
7. Gross motor equipment

PERSONAL CARE ROUTINES

8. Meals/snacks
9. Toileting/diapering
10. Health practices
11. Safety practices

LANGUAGE AND LITERACY

12. Helping children expand vocabulary
13. Encouraging children to use language
14. Staff use of books with children
15. Encouraging children's use of books
16. Becoming familiar with print

LEARNING ACTIVITIES

17. Fine motor
18. Art
19. Music and movement
20. Blocks
21. Dramatic play
22. Nature/science
23. Math materials and activities
24. Math in daily events
25. Understanding written numbers
26. Promoting acceptance of diversity
27. Appropriate use of technology

INTERACTION

28. Supervision of gross motor
29. Individualized teaching and learning
30. Staff-child interaction
31. Peer interaction
32. Discipline

PROGRAM STRUCTURE

33. Transitions and waiting times
34. Free play
35. Whole-group activities for play and learning

the Items are grouped into Subscales, there are aspects of quality that cross areas. For example, the Items *Child-related display* and *Health practices* in the Space and Furnishings Subscale both include Indicators for conversations and/or printed words/reading, which are aspects of the environment more typically considered as relating to Language and Literacy. Because these are conceptual Subscales, and not empirically based, factor analyses have been conducted by the authors and other researchers (see Chapter 3) to explore constructs underlying the Items. The conceptual Subscales and factors derived empirically can be useful in examining different aspects of the environment and perhaps linking to children's developmental outcomes. However, the ECERS authors have always viewed quality as one global construct, and while

Subscales are offered as an organizing frame for the scale, the authors advocate for the use of the total score, and not Subscale scores, in describing classroom quality.

The sequential organization of the Items and Subscale was intentional. Generally, Items that are more readily observable are listed first, as scoring of these Items can be completed earlier during the observation period. Items that require the full 3-hour time sample and should be scored last, namely, those in the Interactions and Program Structure Subscales, are listed last. This organization was designed to support assessors in completing the scale efficiently.

COMPARABILITY

When a revised measure is developed and introduced to end-users, a natural question that arises is how scores on the new version relate to scores on the previous version. Because the ECERS is used in most of the 50 states' quality rating and improvement systems (QRIS), QRIS administrators specifically want to know what implications a change in version might have on quality ratings and whether quality standards, particularly cut scores for levels of quality, should be adjusted. At least three efforts have been conducted to examine how scores on the ECERS-3 relate to scores on the previous version, ECERS-R, to examine comparability of the two measures; these are described below.

Small-Scale Comparability Study in Pennsylvania

As part of the initial field test of the ECERS-3, a sample of 51 preschool classrooms in Pennsylvania was assessed with both the ECERS-R and the ECERS-3. Assessors were highly trained and experienced, and two observers visited a classroom on the same day. One, not familiar with the ECERS-3, completed the ECERS-R; the second, familiar with both tools, completed the ECERS-3. Observations were conducted independently. The classrooms were selected to represent a range of quality levels but were somewhat skewed toward the higher end of quality. Analyses found that average total ECERS-3 scores were nearly 2 points lower, on average, than ECERS-R scores (3.32 vs. 5.18, respectively; see Table 2.1 below). In examining Subscales, the largest average differences between versions were for the Activities and Language Reasoning Subscales. The smallest average difference was found for

Table 2.1. Subscale and Total Scores of ECERS-R and ECERS-3

Subscale	ECERS-R	ECERS-3	Diff.
1. Space/furnishings	4.96	3.51	1.45
2. Personal Care Routines	3.83	3.63	0.20
3. Language Reasoning (Language & Literacy)	5.50	3.29	2.21
4. Activities (Learning Activities)	5.37	2.67	2.70
5. Interaction	5.91	4.12	1.79
6. Program Structure	5.12	3.43	1.69
Total Score	5.18	3.32	1.86

the Personal Care Routines Subscale (0.2-point difference, on average). Many Items in this Subscale were revised to better reflect current standards of care and to make it less likely that classrooms would have difficulty scoring above a 1 or a 2, which was a problem with the ECERS-R, so in fact the revisions meant that providers generally would earn higher scores on individual Items in this Subscale.

Overall, however, the scale authors revised the tool to raise quality standards, so it was expected that scores would likely be lower initially. It was expected that as the tool became more familiar to providers and technical assistance specialists, learning and quality improvement efforts would raise ECERS-3 scores. Using longitudinal data on the ECERS-R and the patterns of improvement that occurred over time, Pennsylvania administrators modeled expected quality improvement on the ECERS-3 after adoption of the new tool to make decisions about recalibration. The graph of that state's ECERS-R scores and hypothetical ECERS-3 improvement is shown below in Figure 2.2 (Clifford, 2015), illustrating that within 3 years of the transition, average ECERS-3 scores would be expected to approach those of the ECERS-R before the transition.

Larger Study in North Carolina

Second, a team of researchers explored comparability between ECERS-R and ECERS-3 in a sample of 105 classrooms in North Carolina (Hestenes et al., 2019). Unlike the Pennsylvania study described above, the North Carolina study involved classroom observations using ECERS-R and ECERS-3 completed on separate days within

Figure 2.2. Longitudinal Quality Improvement and Modeling a Potential Transition From ECERS-R to ECERS-3 Using Data from Pennsylvania

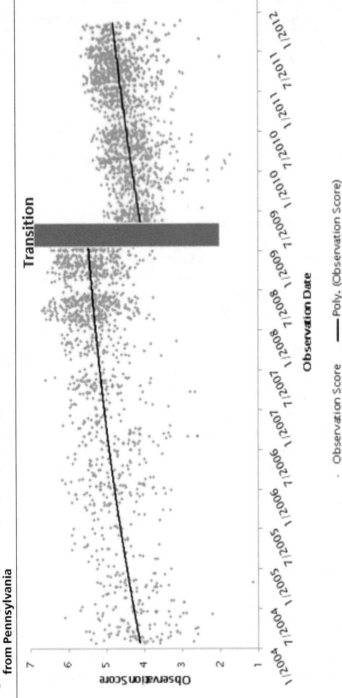

Source: Clifford, 2015.

a 2-week window, for most classrooms (note: 23 of the 105 classrooms were observed on the same day, but the data were not presented separately for this small subset). The researchers found that the correlation between scores on the two scales was .60, which was interpreted as suggesting that the tools were measuring distinct but overlapping aspects of quality (Hestenes et al., 2019). The total score and Subscale means were higher for ECERS-R than ECERS-3, as in the Pennsylvania study reported above. The researchers also examined the lowest-scoring Items for each tool. For the ECERS-R, most of the lowest scoring Items were for health/sanitation or structural aspects of the environment (e.g., safety hazards, access to space, furnishings, materials). For ECERS-3, the lowest-scoring Items were related to teacher–child interactions around learning activities. Finally, the researchers examined associations between the ECERS-R/ECERS-3 scores and structural quality (i.e., ratio, teacher education level, teacher experience at the program). They found that better ratios and higher teacher education (i.e., above an associate's degree) were associated with higher scores on the ECERS-3, but not the ECERS-R. Teachers' length of time at the program was not associated with scores on either tool. The researchers aptly noted that in the state studied (North Carolina), the ECERS-R was extremely familiar to programs because of its use as a high-stakes tool in the quality rating and improvement system. This may have artificially inflated the scores on the day the ECERS-R tool was used as part of that assessment process (i.e., resulted in "quality for a day") and may have blunted any associations with teacher education (Hestenes et al., 2019).

Secondary Analysis of Data from Five States

Finally, a third comparability effort used existing data from five states to examine differences and relations between the ECERS-R and ECERS-3 (Neitzel et al., 2019). This study included scores gathered by different assessors in the same classroom on the same day and subsumed the Pennsylvania sample and a subset of the North Carolina sample, the 23 classrooms observed by two assessors on the same day, described previously. As in the two studies described above, ECERS-R total and Subscale scores were significantly higher than ECERS-3, except for the ECERS-3 Personal Care Routines Subscale which scored slightly higher than the comparable ECERS-R Subscale in this analysis. The correlation between scores on the two scales was modest at .50, which suggests that the tools are measuring some common elements but are distinct tools (Neitzel et al., 2019).

VALIDITY AND RELIABILITY OF PREVIOUS VERSIONS

Before describing analyses of ECERS-3 data, it is useful to note that the validity and reliability of previous versions, ECERS and ECERS-R, have been well established in the literature. The ECERS and ECERS-R have been implemented with reliability as core assessments of child care classroom quality in research, practice, and policy. The ECERS or ECERS-R have been used in nearly all of the most prominent studies related to early education quality, including the following:

- National Child Care Staffing Study (Whitebook et al., 1989)
- Cost, Quality, and Child Outcomes Study (Helburn, 1995)
- National Center on Early Development and Learning's Multi-State Study of Pre-Kindergarten and Study of State-Wide Early Education Programs (Early et al., 2005)
- Early Childhood Longitudinal Study-Birth Cohort (Mulligan & Flanagan, 2006)
- Head Start Family and Child Experiences Survey (FACES; Hulsey et al., 2011)
- Educare Implementation Study (Yazejian et al., 2013)
- Several statewide pre-K evaluations (e.g., Maxwell et al., 2009; Peisner-Feinberg, 2017)

In addition, several states currently use the ECERS as part of their quality rating and improvement systems (QRIS). Across research, practice, and policy applications, the ECERS and ECERS-R have generally been shown to produce scores that are reliable (e.g., scores are consistent across raters and are internally consistent, measuring cohesive constructs) and valid (e.g., relate to other aspects or measures of quality). The scales have also shown some predictive validity in relation to child outcomes, but these associations have been more modest in recent analysis (Burchinal et al., 2011).

Several previous studies using the ECERS have revealed relations between scores and other aspects of structural quality, which provides evidence of concurrent validity. For example, a recent meta-analysis of the literature from 1980 to 2014 found that higher levels of teacher qualifications were associated with higher early care and education quality as measured with the ECERS, ECERS-R, or infant–toddler versions of the scales (Manning et al., 2017). Associations have also been found between ECERS quality scores and other structural features, such as staff-to-child ratios, director education and experience, and wages (Cryer et al., 1999; Helburn, 1995; Vermeer et al., 2016).

Associations have also been reported between ECERS scores and scores on other commonly used process quality measures, providing additional evidence for concurrent validity. Studies have found associations between ECERS and the Caregiver Interaction Scale (CIS; Arnett, 1989), the Classroom Assessment Scoring System—Pre-K (CLASS Pre-K; Pianta et al., 2008), and the Early Literacy and Language Classroom Observation (ELLCO; Smith et al., 2002), with the size of associations generally being moderate (Early et al., 2005; Helburn, 1995; Mayer & Beckh, 2016; Sabol et al., 2013; Weiland et al., 2013). Evidence from a validation study suggests that the ECERS-3 is also moderately related to the CLASS Pre-K (Early et al., 2018).

Finally, studies have provided some evidence of predictive validity of the ECERS with reported associations between scores on the measures and children's developmental outcomes. Research has shown associations between process quality as measured with the ECERS and children's language and literacy (Aboud & Hossain, 2011; Bryant et al., 2003; Burchinal et al., 2000, 2008; Côté et al., 2013; Mashburn et al., 2008; Peisner-Feinberg et al., 2001; Pinto et al., 2013; Sammons et al., 2004), math (Aboud & Hossain, 2011; Anders et al., 2012; Burchinal et al., 2008; Côté et al., 2013; Peisner-Feinberg et al., 2001; Sammons et al., 2004), and social-emotional development (Burchinal et al., 2008; Mashburn et al., 2008; Montes et al., 2005; Peisner-Feinberg et al., 2001). However, recent research has found attenuated associations between process quality measures, including the ECERS, and children's outcomes, suggesting the need for more sensitive measures of quality (Burchinal et al., 2011; Gordon et al., 2013, 2015; Sabol & Pianta, 2014; Sabol et al., 2013; Weiland et al., 2013). With the latest revision, the ECERS-3 was designed with the goal of being more strongly associated with outcomes, and initial evidence from a large-scale validation study of the ECERS-3 suggests some associations with executive function skills, which are considered critically important aspects of children's school readiness (Early et al., 2018).

CHAPTER 3

Summarizing ECERS-3 Data Descriptively

In this chapter, we focus on descriptive statistics—a set of techniques for summarizing and displaying the data from our sample. We look first at some of the most common techniques for describing single variables, followed by some of the most common techniques for describing statistical relationships between variables.

SAMPLE

The data analyzed in this guide come from a large-scale validation study of the ECERS-3 that began in 2015 and was led by Dr. Diane Early, then a scientist at the University of North Carolina at Chapel Hill. The purpose of that study was to analyze the psychometric properties of the ECERS-3 and to explore alternative scoring techniques. The data were gathered in three states—Georgia, Pennsylvania, and Washington—through classroom observations in state-funded pre-K, child care, and Head Start programs. Additional data from these states were added to our data set to increase sample size. The data were gathered electronically using software developed by Branagh Information Group. De-identified data sets were shared for the secondary analyses conducted in this guide. A total of 1,369 classrooms were included in these analyses. Table 3.1 provides numbers of classrooms broken down by program types; note that 526 classrooms were missing information on at least one of the program type variables.

STATISTICAL METHODS

Descriptive statistics refers to a set of techniques for summarizing and displaying data. Let us assume here that the data are quantitative and

Table 3.1. Number of Classrooms in the Sample by Location and Program Type

Located in a Public School Building							
Yes 145				No 698			
Head Start Program							
Yes 22		No 123		Yes 91		No 607	
Pre-K Program							
Yes 7	No 15	Yes 47	No 76	Yes 17	No 74	Yes 227	No 380

consist of scores on one or more variables for each of several study participants. Although in most cases the primary research question will be about one or more statistical relationships between variables, it is also important to describe each variable individually. For this reason, we begin by looking at some of the most common techniques for describing single variables.

Central Tendency

The central tendency of a distribution is its middle—the point around which the scores in the distribution tend to cluster. There are two most common measures of central tendency: mean and median. In sections below we will examine the means of Items and Subscales of the ECERS-3 to see how classrooms scored.

Mean. The mean of a distribution is the sum of the scores divided by the number of scores. The mean is by far the most common measure of central tendency and has statistical properties that make it especially useful in doing inferential statistics:

$$Mean = \frac{\sum_{i=1}^{n} x_i}{n}$$

Median. A small sample size of extremely high or extremely low scores may have a large effect on the mean of a set of scores, so sometimes the use of alternate methods of showing the central tendency is needed. An alternative to the mean is the median. The median is the middle score in the sense that half the scores in the distribution are less than it and half are greater than it. The simplest way to find the median is to organize the scores from lowest to highest and locate the score in the middle.

$$\text{when } n \text{ is odd, } Median = \left(\frac{n+1}{2}\right)^{th} observation$$

$$\text{when } n \text{ is even, } Median = \frac{\left(\frac{n}{2}\right)^{th} observation + \left(\frac{n}{2}+1\right)^{th} observation}{2}$$

Variability

The variability of a distribution is the extent to which the scores vary around their central tendency. A set of scores can have similar central tendencies (e.g., means and/or medians) but have very different distributions around those central values.

Range. One simple measure of variability is the range, which is simply the difference between the highest and lowest scores in the distribution. Although the range is easy to compute and understand, it can be misleading when there are outliers (i.e., a few extreme scores at the high or low end of the distribution).

$$Range = Max - Min$$

Standard Deviation. The most common measure of variability is the standard deviation. The standard deviation of a distribution is the average distance between the scores and the mean. It involves finding the difference between each score and the mean, squaring each difference, finding the mean of these squared differences, and finally finding the square root of that mean. The formula looks like this:

$$Standard\ Deviation = \sqrt{\frac{\sum_{i=n}^{n}\left(x_i - \bar{x}\right)^2}{n-1}}$$

Shape

When the distribution of a quantitative variable is displayed in a density curve, it has a shape. A typical shape has a peak somewhere near the middle of the distribution and "tails" that taper in either direction from the peak. Common distribution shapes are unimodal, meaning they have one distinct peak, and bimodal, meaning they have two distinct peaks. Two other characteristics of the shape of a distribution are whether it is symmetrical or skewed (i.e., skewness) and peaked or narrow (i.e., kurtosis).

Skewness. Skewness assesses the extent to which a variable's distribution is symmetrical (Hair et al., 2016). If the distribution of responses for a variable stretches toward the right or left tail of the distribution, then the distribution is referred to as skewed. A general guideline for the skewness statistic is that if the number is greater than +1 or less than −1, this is an indication of a substantially skewed distribution.

$$Skewness = \frac{n}{(n-1)(n-2)} \sum_{i=1}^{n} \left(\frac{x_i - \bar{x}}{s} \right)^3$$

Kurtosis. Kurtosis is a measure of whether the distribution is too peaked (a very narrow distribution with most of the responses in the center) (Hair et al., 2016). The general guideline is that if the kurtosis score is greater than +1, the distribution is too peaked (i.e., platykurtic). Likewise, a kurtosis score of less than −1 indicates a distribution that is too flat (i.e., leptokurtic).

$$Kurtosis = \left\{ \frac{n(n+1)}{(n-1)(n-2)(n-3)} \sum_{i=1}^{n} \left(\frac{x_i - \bar{x}}{s} \right)^4 \right\} - \frac{3(n-1)^2}{(n-2)(n-3)}$$

DESCRIBING ITEMS

We now turn to applying these statistics that describe variables to ECERS-3 Items. Table 3.2 shows the descriptive statistics of Item scores on the ECERS-3 for the sample of 1,369 early childhood classrooms. While researchers tend to look for relationships between variables, simple descriptive data is often of major use for looking for meaningful information on the sample. The two graphs show separate ways of displaying this data. The first is simple and clear, but the second provides information on the percentage of each score for each Item. The first example may be most useful in describing the scoring to

Table 3.2. Item-Level Descriptive Statistics

Item Labels (Abbreviated)	N	Mean	SD	Minimum	Maximum	Skewness	Kurtosis
Item1_Indoor	1,369	4.52	1.58	1.00	7.00	0.13	−1.01
Item2_Furnishing	1,369	4.06	1.12	1.00	7.00	0.97	1.76
Item3_RoomArrange	1,369	3.36	1.44	1.00	7.00	0.67	−0.14
Item4_Privacy	1,369	4.02	1.61	1.00	7.00	−0.07	−0.53
Item5_Display	1,369	3.26	1.35	1.00	7.00	−0.16	−0.26
Item6_GrossMotSpace	1,369	3.21	1.40	1.00	7.00	0.19	0.16
Item7_GrossMotEquip	1,369	2.88	1.70	1.00	7.00	0.61	−0.73
Item8_Meal	1,369	3.11	1.31	1.00	7.00	0.28	−0.08
Item9_Toileting	1,369	3.16	1.41	1.00	7.00	0.89	0.54
Item10_Health	1,369	3.06	1.43	1.00	7.00	0.47	−0.44
Item11_Safety	1,369	4.01	1.71	1.00	7.00	0.11	−1.07
Item12_Vocabulary	1,369	3.66	1.44	1.00	7.00	0.62	0.24
Item13_EncourageLang	1,369	4.17	1.55	1.00	7.00	0.15	−0.55
Item14_StaffBook	1,369	3.38	1.70	1.00	7.00	0.22	−1.01
Item15_EncourageBook	1,369	3.64	1.45	1.00	7.00	0.34	0.24
Item16_Print	1,369	3.18	1.24	1.00	7.00	0.46	0.03
Item17_FineMotor	1,369	3.93	1.59	1.00	7.00	0.04	−0.79
Item18_Art	1,369	3.40	1.42	1.00	7.00	0.41	0.23
Item19_Music	1,369	3.14	1.17	1.00	7.00	0.23	−0.85
Item20_Blocks	1,369	2.20	1.22	1.00	7.00	0.74	−0.15
Item21_Drama	1,369	3.15	1.64	1.00	7.00	0.54	−0.20
Item22_Science	1,369	2.52	1.18	1.00	7.00	0.85	1.33
Item23_MathAct	1,369	2.28	1.32	1.00	7.00	0.91	0.60
Item24_MathDay	1,369	2.97	1.44	1.00	7.00	0.44	−0.44
Item25_WriteNum	1,369	1.73	1.13	1.00	7.00	2.44	6.73
Item26_Diversity	1,369	4.04	1.21	1.00	7.00	0.50	−0.84
Item27_Technology	375	3.04	1.83	1.00	7.00	0.20	−1.30
Item28_SuperviseGrossMot	1,369	4.08	1.74	1.00	7.00	−0.20	−0.71
Item29_Individualized	1,369	4.24	1.69	1.00	7.00	0.08	−0.64

(*continued*)

Item Labels (Abbreviated)	N	Mean	SD	Minimum	Maximum	Skewness	Kurtosis
Item30_StafChildInteract	1,369	4.95	1.87	1.00	7.00	−0.45	−0.98
Item31_Peer Interaction	1,369	4.44	1.54	1.00	7.00	−0.66	−0.23
Item32_Discipline	1,369	4.16	1.52	1.00	7.00	−0.28	−0.51
Item33_Transitions	1,369	3.84	1.91	1.00	7.00	−0.11	−1.15
Item34_FreePlay	1,369	4.05	1.53	1.00	7.00	−0.03	−0.09
Item35_WholeGroupAct	1,346	3.73	1.52	1.00	7.00	0.05	−0.79

policymakers or the general public. The second may well be useful to program directors or those providing technical assistance to programs wanting to make improvements in quality.

Central Tendency

Figure 3.1 displays the mean for each of the ECERS-3 Items. In the sample analyzed for this guide, the Item with the highest score was *Staff-child interaction* (Item 30), with a mean of 4.95. The next five highest-scored Items were Item 1 *Indoor space* (4.52), Item 31 *Peer Interaction* (4.44), Item 29 *Individualized teaching and learning* (4.24), Item 13 *Encouraging children to use language* (4.17), and Item 32 *Discipline* (4.16). For the sample of state-funded pre-K, child care, and Head Start programs included in this sample, these six Items were relative areas of strength. Four of these Items measured aspects of interactions, suggesting that the classrooms in this sample were particularly strong in meeting children's needs for interpersonal exchanges of various types.

The Item with the lowest score in the sample was Item 25, *Understanding written numbers*, with a mean of 1.73. The next five lowest-scoring Items, all with averages under the minimal level of 3, were Item 20 *Blocks* (2.2), Item 23 *Math materials and activities* (2.28), Item 22 *Nature/science* (2.52), Item 7 *Gross motor equipment* (2.88), and Item 24 *Math in daily events* (2.97). For the sample of programs analyzed for this guide, these six Items were relative areas of need and could be seen as potential targets for professional development or other intervention. Five of the six Items were in learning activities, and more specifically, three of the Items were related to science,

Figure 3.1. Mean ECERS-3 Item Scores

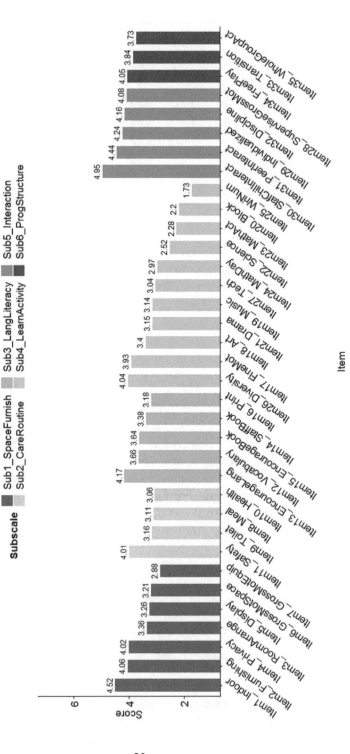

technology, engineering, and math (STEM) learning. This might be an area of particular need in early childhood programs.

Variability

Item 2 *Furnishings for care, play, and learning* (1.12), Item 25 *Understanding written numbers* (1.13), Item 19 *Music and movement* (1.17), and Item 22 *Nature/science* (1.18) had relatively low variability, with the SDs less than 2. Low variability may be an indication of areas that are easier (if mean scores are high) or harder (if mean scores are low). If scores are low, with little variability, it could be that structural factors are serving as barriers for a sample of programs. In cases such as that, a target for improvement may not be professional development but rather policy change at some level of the system within which the programs operate. At the other end in the sample analyzed for this guide, Item 33 *Transitions and waiting times* (1.91), Item 30 *Staff-child interaction* (1.87), and Item 27 *Appropriate use of technology* (1.83) had relatively high variabilities, with the SDs greater than 1.8. These scores indicate that these Items, while low in some cases, may be especially amenable to change, since substantial numbers of classrooms have been able to achieve high scores.

DESCRIBING SUBSCALES

We now move to examining the Subscale and Total Scale scores for the sample. Table 3.3 shows the descriptive statistics of total and Subscale scores on the ECERS-3 for the sample of 1,369 early childhood classrooms.

Central Tendency

In Figure 3.2 we can see that the ECERS-3 Total and Subscales 1, 2, and 3 scores tend to cluster around the value 3.6. The Subscale with the highest score is *Interaction* (Subscale 5), with a mean of 4.38, whereas *Learning Activities* (Subscale 4) has the lowest score, at slightly under 3. It is about a half-point (about 1/2 standard deviation) lower than the next lowest Subscale. Clearly this situation calls for further examination, especially since one would normally think that learning activities are central to several dimensions of children's development. The Subscale with the second-highest score is *Program Structure*

Table 3.3. Total and Subscale-level Descriptive Statistics

Variable	N	Mean	Median	SD	Minimum	Maximum	Skewness	Kurtosis
Total	1,369	3.63	3.61	0.84	1.38	6.04	−0.02	−0.34
1. Space/Furnish	1,369	3.62	3.57	0.78	1.29	6.14	0.08	−0.21
2. Care Routines	1,369	3.34	3.25	0.98	1.00	6.50	0.38	−0.01
3. Language/ Literacy	1,369	3.61	3.6	1.04	1.00	6.80	0.30	−0.07
4. Learning Activities	1,369	2.94	2.9	0.88	1.10	6.18	0.61	0.40
5. Interaction	1,369	4.38	4.4	1.29	1.00	6.80	−0.38	−0.51
6. Prog. Structure	1,369	3.88	4	1.31	1.00	7.00	0.03	−0.68

(Subscale 6), at 3.88. Examining average Subscale scores, like Item scores, helps identify areas of strength and weakness for targeting technical assistance and professional development efforts.

Variability and Shape

Figure 3.3 shows distributions of the overall ECERS-3 scale and each Subscale for the sample of programs analyzed for this guide. The Total score and Subscale 1 (*Space and Furnishings*) are relatively normally distributed—the mean is roughly the same as the median. In the skewed distributions (e.g., Subscales 2–5), the mean differs from the median in the direction of the skewness (i.e., the direction of the longer tail). For the positively skewed distributions of Subscales 2–4, the means are pulled to the right; for the negatively skewed distribution of Subscale 5, the mean is pulled to the left.

Figure 3.3 also illustrates that two distributions can have a similar central tendency but different variability. Subscales 2 and 3 illustrate this: Both have a mean and median of about 3.6, but the two distributions differ in terms of their variability. The Subscale 1 (*Space and Furnishings*) distribution has relatively low variability, with all the scores relatively close to the center (SD = 0.78), while Subscale 3 (*Language and Literacy*) has higher variability, with the scores spread across a much greater range (SD = 1.04). However, interestingly, most of the standard deviation values cluster around 1.0, suggesting that

Figure 3.2. Mean ECERS-3 Rating by Subscale

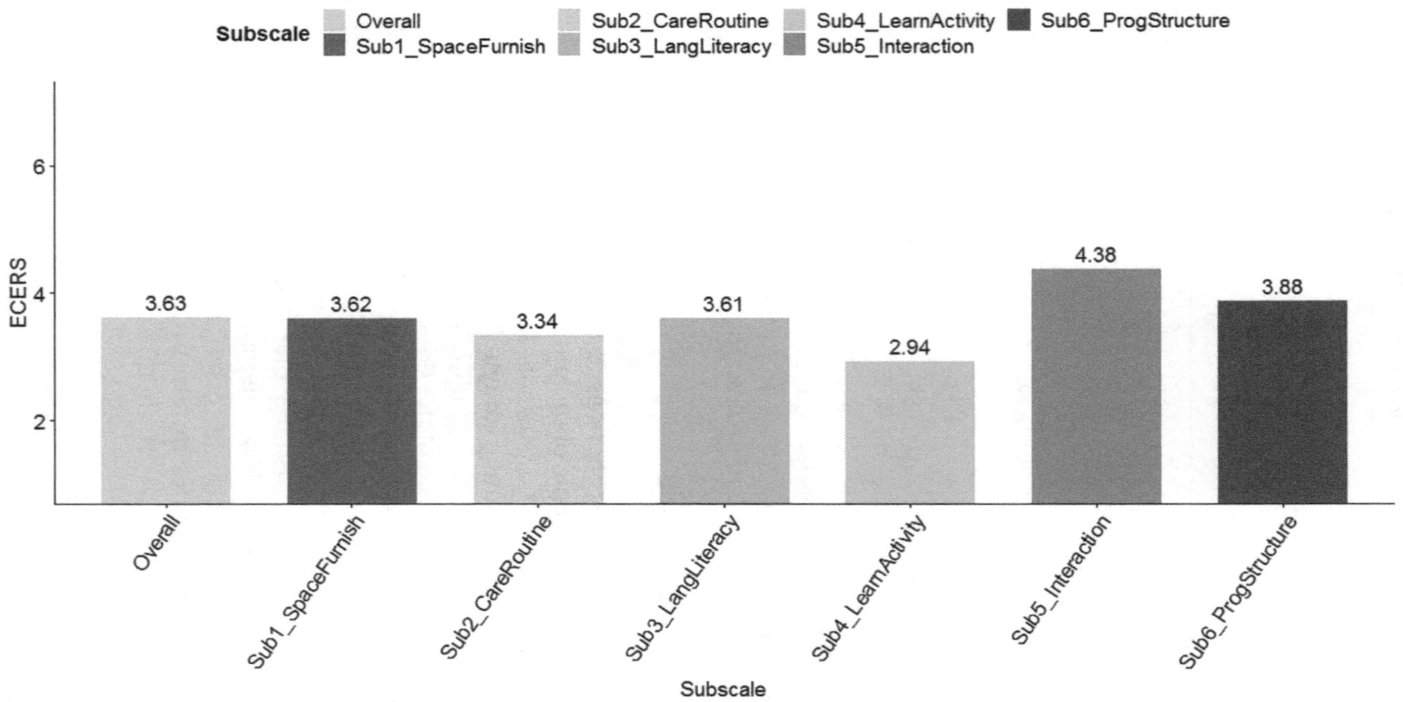

Figure 3.3. Density Curves Showing Central Tendencies, Variabilities, and Shapes

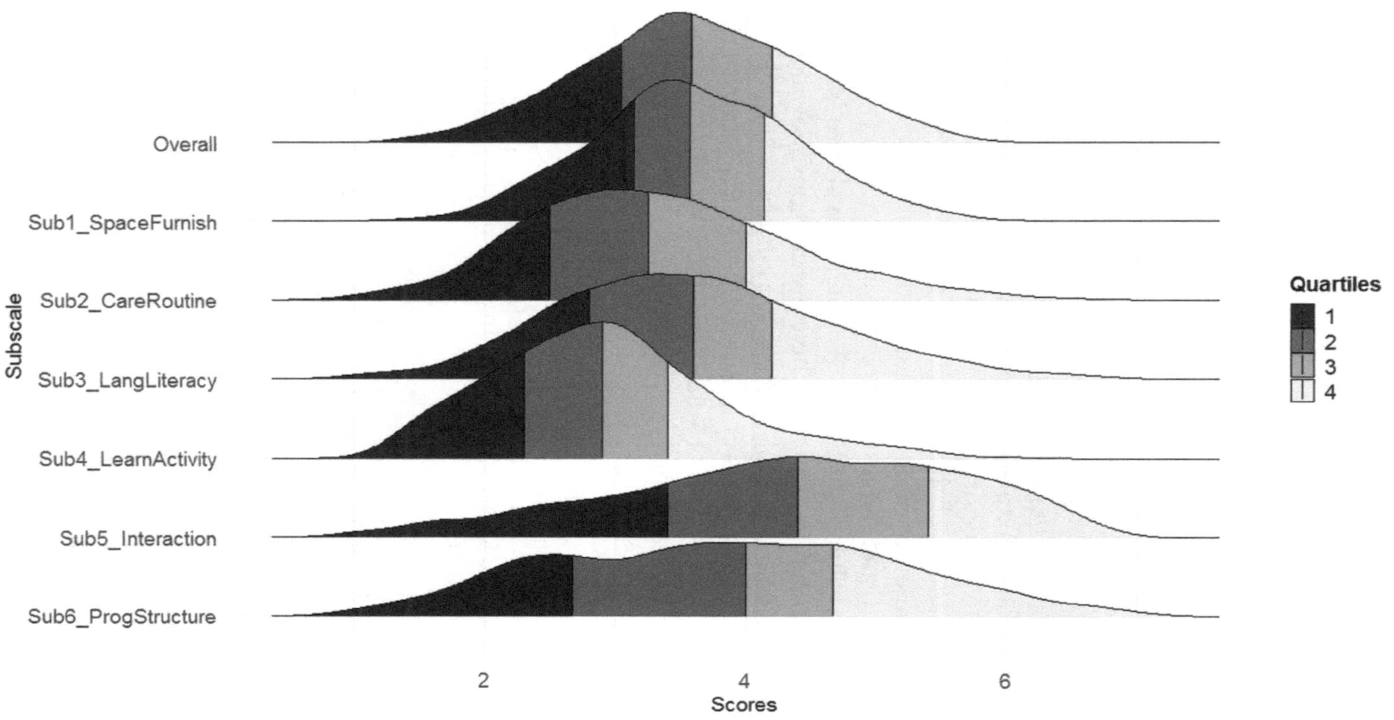

there is enough difference in scores in each Subscale for improvement, and that improvement in scores is attainable. In fact, the range of scores in each Subscale is close to the extremes of the scale. This means that the sample chosen was indeed reaching the full range of classrooms in the population in terms of ECERS-3 scores.

The shape of the distribution of ECERS-3 scores in Figure 3.3 is typical. For each of the Subscales, there is a peak somewhere near the middle of the distribution and "tails" that taper in either direction from the peak. The distributions of Subscales 1–4 are unimodal, meaning that they have one distinct peak; the distributions of Subscales 5 and 6 are bimodal, meaning they have two distinct peaks. In terms of whether the distributions are symmetrical or skewed (i.e., skewness) and peaked or flat (i.e., kurtosis), Figure 3.3 shows that the distributions of Subscales 1 and 6 are symmetrical: the left and right halves are mirror images of each other. On the other hand, the distributions of Subscales 2–4 are positively skewed, and the distribution of Subscale 5 is negatively skewed. The kurtoses values of Subscales 1, 5, and 6, as shown in Table 3.3, are less than zero and in Figure 3.3 these distributions show light tails (i.e., platykurtic), indicating small outliers. The kurtosis of Subscale 4 is greater than zero and it shows heavy tails (i.e., leptokurtic), indicating large outliers. The kurtoses values of Subscales 2 and 3 are close to zero, and normal distribution is assumed (i.e., mesokurtic).

OTHER SUMMARY SCORES

Although the ERS measures have Items that are grouped into seven (original versions) or six (most recent versions) conceptual Subscales, most previous empirical work has suggested that the scores are best represented by either a single factor representing global quality (Perlman et al., 2004) or, as supported by more evidence, by two or three factors (Cassidy et al., 2005; Clifford et al., 2005; Early et al., 2006; Frede et al., 2007; Gordon et al. 2013; Sakai et al., 2003). When analyses have found two factors, Items have generally loaded similarly across analyses and have been labeled as (1) learning activities and materials with Items mainly from the Space and Furnishing, Activities, and Program Structure Subscales and (2) interactions and language facilitation with Items mainly from the Language/Reasoning and Interaction Subscales. When a third factor has been identified, it has been identified as a health and safety factor, with most Items coming from the Personal Care Routines Subscale and single Items from other Subscales measuring safety aspects of the environment. A similar 3-factor solution was recently identified with data from German early education programs (Mayer & Beckh, 2016). All of these studies have looked at factors at the Item level, meaning that the analyses are calculated from Item scores rather than indicator scores.

We conducted analyses of the existing ECERS-3 data set using exploratory factor analysis (EFA). EFA has been employed to build new theory and determine the best factor solution for assessment tools (Watkins, 2018). Particularly, factor rotation simplifies factor structure and therefore makes its interpretation easier and more reliable (i.e., easier to replicate with different data samples) (Cattell, 2012; Thurstone, 1947). Orthogonal rotations of the factor axes have been widely used to maximize the variance of the squared loadings of a factor on all the variables in a factor matrix. Oblique rotations are much less popular than their orthogonal counterparts (Abdi, 2003). In the fields of social sciences, however, requiring factors to be orthogonal (i.e., linearly independent) is often too extreme (Jennrich, 2002). Given the potential correlations among classroom logistics, activities, and interactions, we used promax rotation, which allows factors to be correlated, to explore the best factor structure of the ECERS-3 Items.

To investigate how well the models fit the data (i.e., how close the covariance implied by the EFA is to the covariance estimated directly from the data), global fit indices were used. Thus, if the data are unlikely given the model, then we reject the model (reject the null hypothesis); and if the data are not unlikely, we retain the model (do not reject the null hypothesis). To begin with, Chi-square tests of model fit were used to test the null hypothesis (see Table 3.4). The Chi-square difference test suggests that the 7-factor model may have a significantly better fit than the other models.

To further evaluate the fit of proposed models with our data and determine the best model fit, we used the following Goodness of Fit indices (see Table 3.5): (1) Root Mean Square Error of Approximation (RMSEA) estimates the degree of misfit in a model by rescaling the noncentrality parameter from the Chi-square test; RMSEA values for the 4-, 5-, 6-, and 7-factor models were equal or less than .05, indicating a good model-data fit (Hu & Bentler, 1999); (2) incremental fit indices were used to compare our model (M) to the baseline model (B)—CFI and TLI indices for the 6- and 7-factor models were greater than .95, demonstrating a good fit; (3) for Standardized Root Mean Square Residuals (SRMR), all values were less than .08, suggesting a good fit; however, it should be mentioned that a value of 0 indicates perfect fit (Hu & Bentler, 1999);

Table 3.4. Chi-square Tests of Model Fit

Models Compared	Chi-square	Degrees of Freedom	P-value
2-factor against 3-factor	619.34	27	<0.001
3-factor against 4-factor	361.21	26	<0.001
4-factor against 5-factor	215.23	25	<0.001
5-factor against 6-factor	204.81	24	<0.001
6-factor against 7-factor	140.44	23	<0.001

Table 3.5. Factor Model Goodness of Fit Indices

Indices	2-Factor	3-Factor	4-Factor	5-Factor	6-Factor	7-Factor	Threshold
RMSEA	0.069	0.058	0.05	0.044	0.038	0.032	<0.05
CFI	0.861	0.911	0.939	0.956	0.971	0.981	>0.95
TLI	0.838	0.888	0.917	0.933	0.952	0.965	>0.95
SRMR	0.054	0.039	0.031	0.026	0.022	0.017	<0.08
AIC	93734	93169	92859	92694	92537	92443	-
BIC	94296	93863	93681	93638	93599	93617	-

Note: A blue cell indicates that the index satisfies the threshold value.

and last, (4) the Information Criteria were used to compare the AIC of the 6-factor and 7-factor models to determine which competing model demonstrated the best fit (Huang, P. H., 2017). The 7-factor model had a lower AIC value, indicating that this model was a better fit for the data (the same holds for the values of BIC).

Based on review of fit indices, we can suggest that the 7-factor model demonstrates a better fit for our data compared to other models. The EFA captures the submodels that define the latent variables with these proposed seven factors: (1) indoor space and room arrangement for play and learning are found to go with Indoor Space and Arrangement; (2) gross motor space, equipment, and supervision of gross motor go with Gross-Motor Activities; (3) fine motor, art, music/movement, blocks, dramatic play, nature/science, free play, individualized teaching and learning, promoting acceptance of diversity, and space for privacy go with Learning Activities; (4) toileting/diapering and health practices go with Personal Care Routines; (5) staff-child interactions, peer interactions, discipline, transition and wait times, and whole-group activities for play and learning go with Interactions; (6) helping children expand vocabulary, encouraging children to use language, staff use of books with children,

Figure 3.4. Reconceptualized Classroom Quality Factors

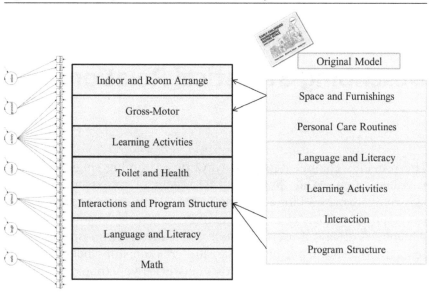

and encouraging children's use of books go with Language and Literacy Activities; and (7) math materials and activities, math in daily events, and understanding written numbers go with Math Activities. However, the final decision about the choice of the best-fit model should rest on human judgment (Hu & Bentler, 1999). Theoretically, the 7-factor model appears to be a reasonable choice because it generates classroom logistics, learning activities, and interactions-related factors and specifies the domain-specific areas such as language and literacy and math (see Figure 3.4). In essence, this new factor structure highlights two aspects of early environments—gross motor and math—as independent factors, rather than being subsumed in other factors. Before accepting the model as the best fit, additional analyses with replication of this factorial structure with different samples as well as a closer examination of relations among the suggested factors and other constructs are needed.

CHAPTER 4

Describing Statistical Relationships

The previous chapter described ways of examining single ECERS-3 variables—Items and Subscales—as a way of understanding how classrooms score and for designing technical assistance or professional development efforts or even regulatory standards. Examining single variables is always a useful place to start. However, most interesting research questions are about statistical relationships between variables. A statistical relationship exists between two variables when the average score on one differs systematically across the levels of the other. In this section, we focus on differences in ECERS-3 scores between groups or conditions and the relationships between quantitative variables. Examinations such as these can help identify subgroups of classrooms or teachers that might have strengths or needs for professional development to improve classroom quality, or to policy changes that would support greater classroom quality for a particular group, such as an agency, community, region, or state.

DIFFERENCES BETWEEN GROUPS OR CONDITIONS

Differences between groups or conditions are usually described in terms of the mean and standard deviation of each group or condition. There are several techniques to look at these differences, as described below.

Analysis of Variance (ANOVA)

Analysis of Variance (ANOVA) determines if there are any statistically significant differences between the means of three or more independent (unrelated) groups. In particular, ANOVA tests if populations have the same mean through comparing how far apart the sample means are with how much variation there is within the samples.

For instance, the one-way between-subjects ANOVA was conducted to look at associations between ECERS-3 total scores and teacher education level (see Figure 4.1). Five groups were included: GED/High School, CDA, Associate's Degree, Bachelor's Degree, and Master's Degree. There was a significant association between teacher education level and ECERS-3 score at the p-value < .001 level for the five conditions [$F(4, 558) = 21.48$, $p < 0.001$]. Post hoc comparisons using the Tukey HSD test indicated that the ECERS-3 mean score for teachers with GED/High School degree (M = 2.96, SD = 0.78) was significantly less than for teachers with Associate's degrees (M = 3.40, SD = 0.72). Moreover, ECERS-3 scores for teachers in the Associate's degree group were significantly lower than those of the Bachelor's degree group (M = 3.72, SD = 0.73). Finally, teachers in the Bachelor's degree group had ECERS-3 scores significantly lower than the those of the Master's degree group (M = 3.96, SD = 0.71). At this level of analysis, teacher education is associated with ECERS-3 scores measuring classroom quality. In Figure 4.1, one sees that each classroom (represented by a dot) falls somewhere along that continuum of ECERS-3 total scores for each of the five levels of teacher education. The bars represent the average or mean score for classrooms within each teacher level of education. The boxes represent two quartiles around the mean—in other words, half (50%) of scores for each teacher education group fall within the boxes. This analysis provides support for increasing the education level of classroom teachers in the sample. In real-life decisionmaking, it is

Figure 4.1. Differences in ECERS-3 Scores by Teacher Education Level

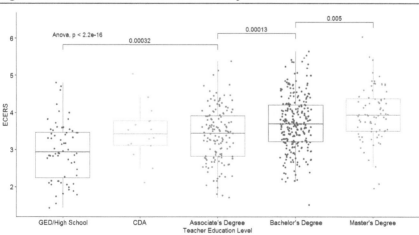

more complicated than this, since we know that teachers with higher levels of education are attracted to different types of programs. In other words, this simple ANOVA does not include other variables that may also be related to both classroom quality and teacher education (e.g., program type).

2^k Factorial Design

Factorial design is a type of statistical testing that allows for the investigation of the main and interaction effects between two or more factors and on one or more outcome variable(s). Particularly, the 2^k factorial design is a special case of the general factorial design: this has k independent variables, each of which has two levels. We used this technique to explore whether there was an association between program type (Head Start, Pre-K) and ECERS-3 total scores.

We found a significant difference in ECERS-3 scores between Head Start (HS) and non-HS classrooms [$F(1, 993) = 18.09, p < 0.001$] and between State Pre-K and non-State Pre-K classrooms [$F(1, 993) = 96.92, p < 0.001$]. In both cases, classrooms that were part of these programs that have more requirements related to quality—for example, standards related to ratios, group size, teacher education, curriculum, assessment—had higher ECERS-3 scores than classrooms that were not part of these programs. However, there was not a significant interaction between the HS and State Pre-K factors [$F(1, 993) = 2.401, p = 0.12$], indicating that the effect of HS does not depend on the State Pre-K status (see Figure 4.2). In general, this set of findings indicates that programs subjected to higher standards are rated as higher quality than programs with less well-developed standards. So, in these states, administrators and policymakers can have confidence that higher standards in their states are having the desired effect on quality as measured by ECERS-3 and that even higher standards could further improve quality. Federal officials in the Head Start program can further see that the relatively high Head Start standards are associated with higher quality, particularly in comparison with non-Pre-K programs. These findings support efforts to raise the standards for programs that are neither State Pre-K nor Head Start.

Correlation

Correlation is a measure of the strength of a linear relation between two numeric variables, whether causal or not. A correlation can only

Figure 4.2. 2 x 2 Factorial Design

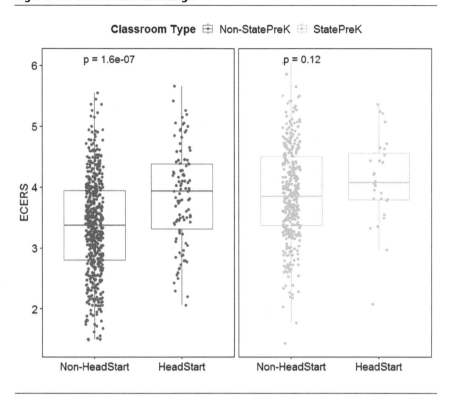

range from −1 to 1: a positive correlation is a relation between two variables in which an increase in one variable is related to an increase in the other, and in a negative correlation, an increase in one variable is related to a decrease in the other. A correlation coefficient of .10 is considered to represent a weak or small association; a correlation coefficient of .30 is considered a moderate correlation; and a correlation coefficient of .50 or larger is considered to represent a strong or large correlation.

All of the ECERS-3 Subscales are positively correlated with each other. The correlation between Subscales 1 and 2, Subscales 2 and 3, and Subscales 2 and 6 show moderate correlations (i.e., r < 0.5), whereas the other correlations show strong correlations (i.e., r > 0.5). These correlations are shown in Figure 4.3, which includes a visual of the correlation, the distribution/shape of each Subscale score, and the numeric value of the correlation coefficient. The adage that good things go together appears to apply to the different ECERS-3 factors.

Figure 4.3. Correlations

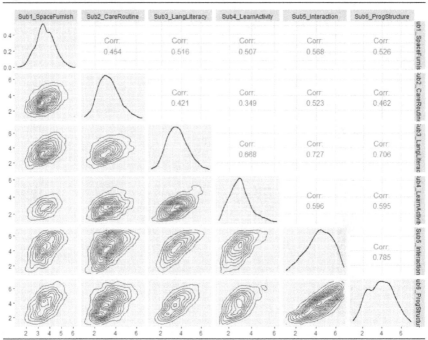

This finding also lends support to the idea that there is some underlying characteristic of programs that cuts across the Subscales—this is what we call global quality, even though it may not be as clearly delineated as we would like. Efforts to improve any of these dimensions of quality are likely to improve other dimensions as well.

SUMMARY

These descriptive methods describing relations between variables are straightforward. Yet they all provide clues for how programs in these three states could address the issue of improving the quality of early education and care. They all can be helpful in allocating scarce resources to almost unlimited needs (Gallagher, 2015) as we seek to improve programs for all children.

CHAPTER 5

Examining Predictors of Quality
Structural Equations Modeling

The existing data set analyzed for this guide included a subset of programs classified as Head Start or State Pre-K programs. As we presented in Chapter 4, descriptive analyses revealed that both Head Start and State Pre-K programs were rated higher in quality as measured with the ECERS-3 than programs that were not Head Start or Pre-K, and that Head Start and Pre-K were not rated significantly different from each other. We interpreted this as suggesting that the regulations and program standards that govern Head Start and State Pre-K (e.g., standards for ratios, group sizes, teacher education, curricula), although different from one another, were serving their intended purpose of maintaining higher quality levels.

For this chapter, we conducted a set of inferential analyses to explore this question more deeply with respect to the Head Start programs in the sample. We tested the notion that Head Start programming led to differences in aspects of those classroom settings associated with variations in quality as measured by the ECERS-3. We begin with a brief description of Head Start, then describe the methods and results of these analyses, and end with some applications and implications for the field.

HEAD START

Established in 1965 as one of President Lyndon B. Johnson's "War on Poverty" initiatives, Head Start is now the largest federal program administered by the U.S. Department of Health and Human Services that serves the developmental needs of low-income children from birth to age 5 and their families (Hinitz, 2014). At a current cost of roughly $7 billion per year, Head Start is designed to serve the "whole

child" through educational, health, nutritional, and parental involvement services (McWayne et al., 2009). Head Start, however, has been
an ongoing source of controversy and continues to be actively debated, with periodic proposals for its expansion or dissolution (Bloom &
Weiland, 2015; The White House, 2013). It should be noted that as of
the writing of this chapter, the future of Head Start, Pre-K, and child
care are under discussion in Congress and in the field. It is almost
certain that the above figures for Head Start, Pre-K, and other early
childhood programs will change significantly over the next few years.

    While a substantial literature has examined the short-term and
long-term effects of Head Start on child, youth, and young adult development (Bloom & Weiland, 2015; Deming, 2009; Ludwig & Miller,
2007; Shager et al., 2013), little has been done to ascertain the extent
to which classroom quality is related to teacher and classroom characteristics that are often mandated by the Head Start Act (Pianta et al.,
2005; Schilder & Leavell, 2015). The analyses conducted for this chapter
are an innovative examination of the nature, magnitude, and patterns
of variation in quality of Head Start and non–Head Start classrooms.

METHODS

To provide new insights about policies surrounding classroom quality, this study used methodological approaches not previously used in
examining such relationships. For explaining the nested nature of our
data (classrooms within states), we used multilevel structural equation modeling (MSEM). For this analysis, we used ECERS-3 observations conducted in a subset of the larger data set examined in the
previous chapter, namely, 327 preschool classrooms across the three
states identified as Head Start classrooms. The approach focused on
classrooms at Level 1 and controlled for the effects of states at Level 2.
Using this approach, our analytic strategy tested if the effect of Head
Start on classroom quality factors was plausibly mediated by structural
components of teachers and classrooms.

    It is crucial to note that the resulting indirect effects cannot be in-
terpreted as causal. This analysis does not examine if Head Start caused
changes in structural components of teachers and classrooms that in
turn caused changes in classroom quality factors. Such an approach
(i.e., causal mediation) requires the assumption of "sequential ignor-
ability," or that assignment to the treatment and then the mediator
are random conditional on pretreatment covariates (Imai et al., 2010).

Although the treatment is randomly assigned and hence ignorable in a randomized control trial, the mediator is not randomly assigned. In this case, it is not empirically testable that there are unobserved variables confounding the association between the mediator and the outcome (Aber et al., 2017). Because of the untestable assumptions that cannot be fully assessed in the current context, we cannot causally interpret the indirect effects.

Despite these limitations, the present analysis allows us to assess whether Head Start caused changes in structural components of teachers and classrooms that are in turn associated with classroom quality factors. Since such associations are a precondition for causal mediation, we consider evidence of such pathways as "plausibly causal." To assess these pathways, we utilized MPlus v7.3 to fit the model that included direct and indirect paths from Head Start to classroom quality factors via structural components of teachers and classrooms. The quality factors analyzed for this exploration were the reconceptualized classroom quality factors described in Chapter 3 (see Figure 3.4).

ASSOCIATIONS AMONG QUALITY AND THREE FEATURES OF CLASSROOMS

According to the Head Start Act (U.S. Department of Health and Human Services, 2017), "A program must ensure teachers implement developmentally appropriate schedules" (p. 27). Based on the statement, Head Start session options generally include a 7-hour or 9-hour day (Family Development Services, 2021). As shown in Figure 5.1, in the sample analyzed for this guide, on average, Head Start classrooms had shorter length of day/operating hours (M = 8.07, SD = 2.39) than Non–Head Start classrooms (M = 9.93, SD = 2.92).

In this context, Head Start caused a significantly shorter length of day. In turn, there was an association between shorter length of day and higher-quality scores for five of the ECERS-3 factors presented in Chapter 3—Indoor and Room Arrangement, Learning Activities, and Language and Literacy (see Table 5.1).

The Head Start Act (U.S. Department of Health and Human Services, 2017) also requires that each Head Start grant maintain at least 10% of all slots occupied by children with disabilities. In the sample analyzed for this guide, as shown in Figure 5.2, Head Start classrooms had a higher proportion of children with disabilities (M = 0.12, SD = 0.12) than Non–Head Start classrooms (M = 0.06, SD = 0.10).

Figure 5.1. Length of Day (Hours) for Head Start and Non–Head Start Programs

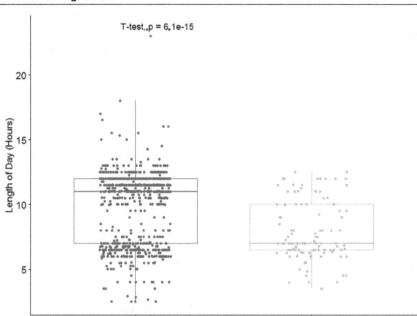

Table 5.1. Results of Multilevel Structural Equation Model Testing the Indirect Effect of Head Start on Classroom Quality Factor Scores Through Changes in Length of Day

Indirect Effect	Estimate	SE	P-value
HEAD START → Length of Day → INDOOR	0.193	0.069	0.005**
HEAD START → Length of Day → ACTIVITY	0.204	0.064	0.002**
HEAD START → Length of Day → LANG_LIT	0.296	0.084	<0.001**
HEAD START → Length of Day → MATH	0.164	0.064	0.01*
HEAD START → Length of Day → INTERACT	0.141	0.056	0.011*

*** $p<.001$; ** $p<.01$; * $p<.05$

Head Start caused significant increases in the proportion of children with disabilities, which in turn were positively associated with the quality factors of Indoor and Room Arrangement and Learning Activities (see Table 5.2).

Finally, the U.S. Department of Health and Human Services (2017) requires that "a program must ensure all center-based teachers have at

Figure 5.2. Proportion of Children With Disabilities in Head Start and Non–Head Start Classrooms

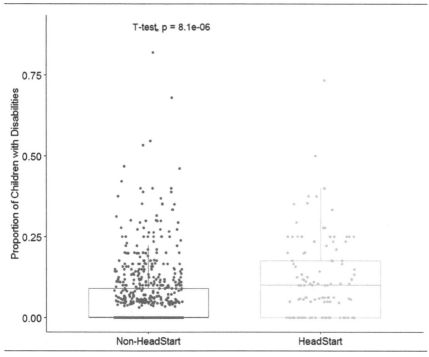

Table 5.2. Results of Multilevel Structural Equation Model Testing the Indirect Effect of Head Start on Classroom Quality Factor Scores Through Changes in Proportion of Children With Disabilities

Indirect Effect	Estimate	SE	P-value
HEAD START → Proportion of Children with Disabilities → INDOOR	0.097	0.049	0.047*
HEAD START → Proportion of Children with Disabilities → ACTIVITY	0.075	0.039	0.055+

* p < .05; + p < .1

least an associate's or bachelor's degree in child development or early childhood education" (p. 55). Head Start caused significant increases in teachers' education level. In turn, there is a small and marginally significant positive association between classroom teachers' education levels and Interaction and Language and Literacy quality factor scores (see Table 5.3).

Table 5.3. Results of Multilevel Structural Equation Model Testing the Indirect Effect of Head Start on Classroom Quality Factor Scores Through Changes in Lead Teacher's Education Level

Indirect Effect	Estimate	SE	P-value
HEAD START → Lead Teacher's Education Level → INTERACT	0.084	0.052	0.103+
HEAD START → Lead Teacher's Education Level → LANG_LIT	0.088	0.054	0.104+

+ p~.1

APPLICATIONS AND IMPLICATIONS

The analyses reported in this chapter demonstrated a technique for determining whether Head Start standards are related to quality factors as measured with the ECERS-3. We found that three structural aspects of classrooms governed by Head Start standards—namely, length of day, proportion of children with disabilities, and lead teacher education levels—were associated with ECERS-3 quality factors. Programs with higher standards—including those that limit the length of day/number of operating hours, include children with disabilities with appropriate supports, and require greater levels of education for lead teachers—tend to have higher quality.

In a more general sense, these findings demonstrate that broad public policies in the form of standards and regulations are effective in achieving higher quality in early childhood programs. The regulation of teacher education requirements is shown here to have a small effect on program quality. Previous research has shown that even higher levels of education that result in formal degrees and certification in early education and development are related to higher-quality classrooms and better child developmental outcomes (Pianta et al., 2005). It is possible that the small associations with teacher education may reflect that Head Start is not as far along in improving teacher qualifications that result in clearly higher quality at this point. This type of regulatory change is expensive but shows promise of making lasting change in the early childhood education field. The analysis demonstrates that length of day for Head Start, which is more closely aligned with typical school hours, affects quality. Another way of stating this is that the substantially longer hours of operation for non–Head Start programs is associated with lower quality. This finding indicates that there are real trade-offs between the longer operating hours to accommodate working families' needs and the program quality that children experience. These trade-offs should be considered in terms of what they mean for the children of those families.

The finding that shorter total time in programs—that is, less than what is considered a full working day, and more in line with traditional school days—offers a policy option that has not been widely recognized. Such a change would face resistance from families with adults working and/or commuting long hours that require them to have extended care for their children. One option to consider under these circumstances is to separate out the educational part of the day from extended care, similar to what is offered in some public and private school settings. The kind of modeling used in this study provides new ways of teasing out the complex relationships between policies and their impact on desired outcomes for children and families.

If we are indeed going to have a more robust and impactful early childhood care and education system in the United States, we will need to look broadly at how programs are governed, regulated, and funded. Much of this work will be the responsibility of state and local officials. Close working relationships between these officials and researchers/evaluators can facilitate and maximize positive results while avoiding unintended consequences associated with moving toward a true system of early childhood services.

CHAPTER 6

Examining Predictors of Quality
Hierarchical Linear Models

In this chapter (and in the supplementary material in the Appendix), we take a more fine-grained look at the relationship between the ECERS-3 Subscales as described earlier and structural characteristics of classrooms. We examine the following program measures: length of day, teacher/child ratio, age differences, proportion of children who are Black, proportion of children who are Hispanic, proportion of children with disabilities, lead teacher education, and lead teacher experience. Inferential analyses were conducted using 2-level hierarchical linear model (HLM) analyses. Separate HLM models were conducted for each Subscale. Within each model, Level 1 described classroom quality as a function of its structural characteristics. In the data set, classrooms are nested within states, and this is represented by random-effects state intercepts. Separate analyses for each outcome tested the extent to which classroom quality was related to Level 1 structural quality characteristics. Main effects for these variables were tested. The unconditional model, without any predictors, is represented by the following equations.

MODEL 1: UNCONDITIONAL MODEL

Level-1 model:

$$ECERS_{ij} = \beta_{0j} + r_{ij}$$

Level-2 model:

$$\beta_{0j} = \gamma_{00} + u_{0j}$$

$$e_{ij} \sim N(0, \sigma^2)$$

In this model, $ECERS_{ij}$ is the outcome variable for classroom i in state j; γ_{00} represents level-2 coefficients (fixed effects); e_{ij} is a level-1 random effect; u_{0j} is a level-2 random effect.

The overall ECERS-3 score in three states was 3.62 ($=\gamma_{00}$), measured with a standard error of 0.13 (p=0.001). The state intercepts do vary (i.e., the square root of the variance [τ_{00}] is 0.22) and, from the chi-square test, this variation in intercepts is confirmed to be significant (p<0.001). The proportion of variance in ECERS-3 scores between states is 7.02% (=ICC). In this sample of three states, significant effects were associated with which state the classroom was located in and classroom quality, as measured by ECERS-3. However, the size of the effect was only modest. We next examined a model with structural characteristics as predictors of quality. The equations for this model are presented below.

MODEL 2: RANDOM-INTERCEPT MODEL

Level-1 model:

$$ECERS_{ij} = \beta_{0j} + \beta_{1j}\,OpenHours_{ij} + \beta_{2j}\,TchChiRatio_{ij} + \beta_{3j}\,AgeDif_{ij}$$
$$+ \beta_{4j}\,PropBlack_{ij} + \beta_{5j}\,PropHisp_{ij}$$
$$+ \beta_{6j}\,PropDisabilities_{ij} + \beta_{7j}\,LTeacherEdu_{ij}$$
$$+ \beta_{8j}\,LTeacherExperience_{ij} + r_{ij}$$

Level-2 model:

$$\beta_{0j} = \gamma_{00} + u_{0j},\ \beta_{1j} = \gamma_{10},\ \beta_{2j} = \gamma_{20},\ \beta_{3j} = \gamma_{30},$$
$$\beta_{4j} = \gamma_{40},\ \beta_{5j} = \gamma_{50},\ \beta_{6j} = \gamma_{60},\ \beta_{7j} = \gamma_{70},\ \beta_{8j} = \gamma_{80}$$
$$e_{ij} \sim N(0,\ \sigma^2),\ u_{0j} \sim N(0,\ \tau^2)$$

In this model, $ECERS_{ij}$ is the outcome variable for classroom i in state j; length of day ($OpenHours_{ij}$), teacher/child ratio ($TchChiRatio_{ij}$), age differences of children in the classroom ($AgeDif_{ij}$), proportion of Black children ($PropBlack_{ij}$), proportion of Hispanic children ($PropHisp_{ij}$), proportion of children with disabilities ($PropDisabilities_{ij}$), lead teacher education level ($LTeacherEdu_{ij}$), and lead teacher experience ($LTeacherExperience_{ij}$) were level-1 variables; γ_{00} is a level-2 coefficient (fixed effects); and $\gamma_{10}, \gamma_{20}, \gamma_{30}, \gamma_{40}, \gamma_{50}, \gamma_{60}, \gamma_{70}$ and γ_{80} are coefficients of the level-1 variables.

Table 6.1. Model 2 Outcome Table

Fixed Effect B (se)	Overall	Sub1_ Space Furnish	Sub2_ Care Routine	Sub3_ Lang Literacy	Sub4_ Learn Activity	Sub5_ Interaction	Sub6_ Prog Structure
Base	3.47*** (0.33)	3.20*** (0.28)	3.15* (0.54)	3.97*** (0.34)	2.96*** (0.28)	4.10** (0.52)	3.41*** (0.42)
Length of Day	-0.07*** (0.01)	-0.03* (0.01)	-0.03+ (0.01)	-0.11*** (0.01)	-0.07*** (0.01)	-0.08*** (0.02)	-0.09*** (0.02)
Teacher/child Ratio	1.85** (0.67)	0.75 (0.69)	0.99 (0.82)	2.41** (0.84)	1.10 (0.75)	2.34* (1.03)	3.40** (1.11)
Age Difference	0.00 (0.00)	0.00 (0.00)	-0.00 (0.00)	-0.00 (0.00)	0.00 (0.00)	0.00 (0.00)	0.00 (0.00)
Prop Black	0.01 (0.15)	0.00 (0.15)	0.18 (0.18)	-0.37* (0.18)	0.23 (0.16)	-0.09 (0.23)	0.12 (0.25)
Prop Latinx	-0.04 (0.20)	0.32 (0.20)	0.54* (0.24)	-0.48+ (0.25)	-0.10 (0.22)	-0.07 (0.31)	-0.45 (0.33)
Prop Disabilities	0.33 (0.31)	0.47 (0.32)	0.52 (0.38)	-0.13 (0.39)	0.20 (0.35)	0.48 (0.48)	0.44 (0.52)
L Teacher Edu	0.14*** (0.03)	0.14*** (0.03)	0.07+ (0.04)	0.15*** (0.04)	0.08* (0.03)	0.16*** (0.05)	0.21*** (0.05)
L Teacher Experience	0.00 (0.00)	0.00 (0.00)	0.00 (0.00)	0.00* (0.00)	0.00 (0.00)	0.00+ (0.00)	0.00 (0.00)

*** $p < 0.001$, ** $p < 0.01$, * $p < 0.05$, + $p < 0.1$

Results of the model are shown in Table 6.1. Classrooms with a longer length of day had significantly lower ECERS-3 scores ($B=-0.07$, se $=0.01$). We performed further analysis using Generalized Additive Modeling (GAM; Hastie & Tibshirani, 1987) to better understand the extent to which length of day and classroom quality are associated. ECERS-3 scores were generally higher around the 6–7 hours length-of-day and then plateaued with decreases over 9 hours. This finding corroborates previous findings that short-day programs tended to have lower scores on classroom quality (Pianta et al., 2005). However, excessively long hours are related to lower quality (see Figure 6.1).

Classrooms with lower teacher/child ratios had significantly higher ECERS-3 scores ($B=1.85$, se $=0.67$, $p<0.01$). Especially, classrooms with lower teacher/child ratios have significantly higher Language and Literacy ($B=2.41$, se $=0.84$, $p<0.01$), Interaction ($B=2.34$, se $=1.03$, $p<0.05$), and Program Structure ($B=3.40$, se $=1.11$, $p<0.01$) Subscale scores. This is consistent with the previous findings that smaller teacher/child ratios were related to higher-quality teacher–child interactions as measured by warmth, sensitivity, and cognitive stimulation (Bowne et al., 2017; NICHD ECCRN, 2002; Phillipsen et al., 1997).

Classrooms with lead teachers who had higher educational levels also had significantly higher ECERS-3 scores ($B=0.14$, se $=0.03$, $p<0.001$). The variability in ECERS-3 scores between states (i.e., the

Figure 6.1. Generalized Additive Modeling

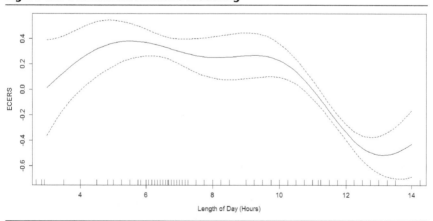

Note: The dashed confidence bands define the confidence interval of the best-fit line; the data points are spread along the x axis. Very few programs operate less than about 5 hours or more than 14 hours per day, so the estimates at the ends of the graph should be interpreted with caution.

square root of the variance [τ]) was 0.34. And from the chi-square test, this variation in intercepts was found to be significant ($p < 0.001$). Note that the residual variance is now 0.48, compared to the residual variance of 0.68 in the one-way ANOVA with random-effects (unconditional means) model. We can compute the proportion variance explained at level 1 as $(0.68–0.48) / 0.68 = .29$. This suggests that using structural characteristics as predictors of ECERS-3 reduced the within-state variance by 29%.

In the analyses described above, we focused on the findings replicated across multiple Subscales. At the individual Subscale level there are three significant findings, but these do not lead to significant findings for the variable for the full ECERS-3 quality score. For classrooms with higher proportions of Black children enrolled, the Language and Literacy Subscale was lower ($B = -0.37$, se $= 0.18$), but while not significant, three of the other Subscale scores showed a tendency toward higher scores, explaining the null effect for the full ECERS-3. Similarly, the proportion of Hispanic/Latinx children in the classroom showed no overall effect on quality, but there was a positive relationship with Personal Care Routines ($B = .54$, se $= 0.24$, $p < 0.05$) and a negative relationship with Language and Literacy Subscales ($B = -0.48$, se $= 0.25$, $p < 0.05$).

Also, if teachers are more experienced, classrooms show higher Language and Literacy ($B = 0.0009$, se $= 0.0004$, $p < 0.05$) and Interaction ($B = 0.0008$, se $= 0.0005$, $p < 0.05$) Subscale scores. While the relationships are quite small, they are significant; thus, our study does support previous findings that more years of teaching experience were positively associated with oral language activities and instructional quality (Berliner, 1986; LoCasale-Crouch et al., 2007; NICHD Early Child Care Research Network, 2002; Rivkin et al., 2005).

SENSITIVITY ANALYSIS USING LASSO

We next verified how "sensitive" the models were to fluctuations in the parameters and data on which they were built. Sensitivity analyses include a series of confirmatory methods to measure the appropriateness of a particular model specification, through quantifying how the uncertainty in the output of a model is relevant to the uncertainty in its inputs (Salciccioli et al., 2016; Saltelli et al., 2000). We used sensitivity analysis to explore whether and how specific parameter values with potentially high uncertainty may have had a critical effect on the model output.

We explored the possibility that our model omitted important interaction and quadratic terms among the structural quality variables using the Least Absolute Shrinkage and Selection Operator (LASSO) approach. LASSO, one of the machine learning techniques most familiar to social scientists, is used to enhance the precision and interpretability of regression models by changing the model fitting process to identify the best-fitting subset of the provided covariates in the final model (Santosa & Symes, 1986; Tibshirani, 1996). As a regularized (penalized) regression method, LASSO uses an ℓ_1 penalty for both fitting and penalization of the coefficients based on Breiman's nonnegative garrote (Breiman, 1995). Unlike ridge regression, which improves prediction error by shrinking large regression coefficients but does not perform covariate selection, LASSO is able to achieve both of these goals by forcing the sum of the absolute value of the regression coefficients to be less than a fixed value, which forces certain coefficients to be set to zero, effectively choosing a simpler model that does not include those coefficients (Gunes, 2015; Hastie et al., 2015).

$$e^2 = \sum_{i=1}^{N} \left(y_i - \hat{y}_i\right)^2 + \lambda \sum_{j=1}^{p} \left|\hat{\beta}_j\right|$$

$$\text{subject to } \sum_{j=1}^{p} \left|\beta_j\right| \leq t$$

In our case, we used LASSO and a validation data approach, which determines a tuning parameter λ, the amount of shrinkage, to look at interactions among the various measures of structural quality to find the best-fitting model that allows for two-way and quadratic interactions (see Figure 6.2). Although this technique has been criticized for yielding outputs that were unreliable and difficult to translate (because of the multicollinearity between the multiplicative terms and its constituent variables), an interactive model can provide accurate and more detailed information about the relations among the variables in the models, increase explanatory power, and improve the prospects for statistically significant results (Afshartous & Preston, 2011; Friedrich, 1982).

The LASSO approach retains some nonsignificant interactions, and these have been deleted to simplify interpretation. This sensitivity analysis is designed to confirm whether the same main effects emerge and to identify potential higher-order terms to be explored in future

Figure 6.2. LASSO Coefficient Estimates and Tuning Parameters

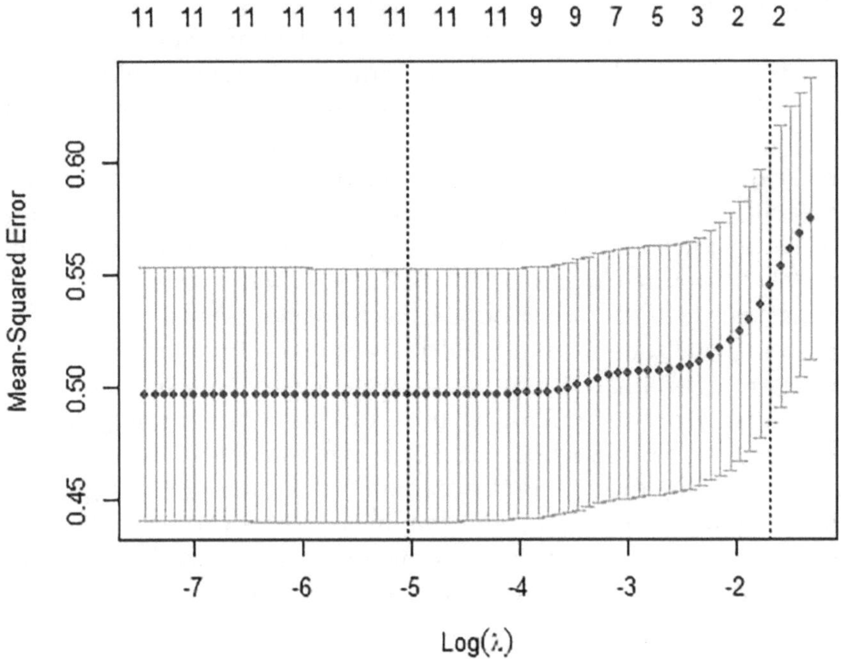

Note: The amount of penalty (λ) giving the minimum Mean-Squared Error (MSE) was found by cross-validation, which is based on finding the optimal balance between bias and variance to establish the most predictive model. The figure contains a cross-validation curve (red dotted line) and the number of variables across the top. The first dotted line is the λ resulting in the lowest MSE, and the second dotted line is the λ within one standard error of the minimum. It is recommended to employ the λ that is within one standard error of the minimum.

studies. The results from the LASSO analyses are shown in Table 6.2. Compared with the HLM analyses described above, these analyses yielded some, but not all, of the same significant associations between structural quality dimensions and ECERS-3 scores. They also suggested some interactions that should be considered in future work. Given the ad hoc nature of these analyses, we focus on the findings that are consistent with the first set of analyses.

First, we found that ECERS-3 scores were negatively associated with length of day, but an interaction effect suggested that the negative association was less strong in classrooms with a greater proportion of children with disabilities (see Figure 6.3). This finding indicates that higher proportions of children with disabilities (i.e., more inclusive

Table 6.2. LASSO Model Outcome Table

Fixed Effect B (se)	Model 1	Model 2
Base	3.72*** (0.34)	3.16*** (0.35)
OpenHours	−0.10*** (0.02)	−0.06*** (0.01)
TchChiRatio	1.80** (0.67)	1.29+ (0.80)
AgeDif	0.00 (0.00)	0.00 (0.00)
PropBlack	0.00 (0.15)	0.09 (0.16)
PropHisp	−0.06 (0.20)	−0.08 (0.21)
PropDisabilities	−2.14* (1.00)	0.58+ (0.36)
LTeacherEdu	0.13*** (0.03)	0.18*** (0.04)
LTeacherExperience	0.00 (0.00)	0.00 (0.00)
PhysicAtElem		1.14* (0.45)
OpenHours*PropDisabilities	0.28** (0.11)	
LTeacherEdu*PhysicAtElem		−0.30* (0.12)

*** p < 0.001, ** p < 0.01, * p < 0.05, + p < 0.1

Figure 6.3. Interaction Effects of Length of Day and Proportion of Children With Disabilities in Predicting ECERS-3 Scores

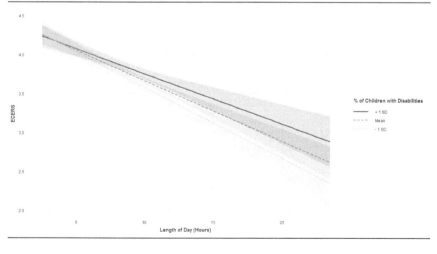

Figure 6.4. Interaction Effects of Teacher Education Level and Classroom Location in Predicting ECERS-3 Scores

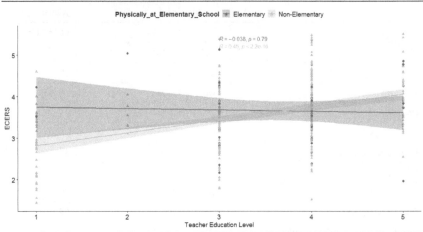

classrooms) may mitigate the negative association between classroom quality and length of day. Second, we found that higher lead teacher educational levels were positively related to ECERS-3 scores when early childhood classrooms were not located in elementary school buildings, indicating that classroom quality is related to teachers' educational levels when classrooms are in nonschool settings (see Figure 6.4).

CHAPTER 7

Examining Groups With Shared Characteristics

From Chapter 4, we know that populations of early childhood programs are often divided into groups or subpopulations; yet these divisions may be inherently unobservable. For example, there may be types of classrooms that share characteristics, but these characteristics are not readily observable. In this case, we can use a statistical technique called finite mixture models (FMM) to model the probability of belonging to each unobserved group, and to estimate distinct parameters of a regression model or distribution in each group. FMM provide for great flexibility in fitting models with many modes, skewness, and nonstandard distributional characteristics (Melnykov & Maitra, 2010). We used FMM with the Expectation-Maximization (EM) algorithm to approximate complex probability densities of groupings of classrooms that have commonalities related to ECERS-3 Subscale scores.

The results revealed seven classroom quality patterns based on ECERS-3 Subscale scores (see Table 7.1 and Figure 7.1). Group 1 (6% of sample) is characterized by relatively high scores across all Subscales except Personal Care Routines (Subscale 2). Group 2 (8% of the sample) is characterized by low scores across all Subscales, while group 3 (8% of the sample) had relatively higher scores in Space and Furnishings (Subscale 1) and Personal Care Routines (Subscale 2). Group 4 (26% of the sample) had mediocre scores across Subscales, with scores ranging from 2.6 to 3.7. Groups 5 (16% of sample), 6 (28% of sample), and 7 (8% of sample) were characterized by high scores in Interactions (Subscale 5) and Program Structure (Subscale 6) and relatively lower scores in Learning Activities (Subscale 4). However, group 6 was characterized by somewhat lower scores in Personal Care Routines (Subscale 2), while group 7 had generally low scores in Space and Furnishings (Subscale 1).

Table 7.1. Gaussian Finite Mixture Models Fitted by EM Algorithm

Group	Percentage	Space_Furnish	Care_Routine	Language_Literacy	Learning_Activity	Interact	Program_Structure
1	6%	4.38	3.91	5.41	4.65	5.81	5.44
2	8%	2.68	2.22	2.19	2.09	2.00	2.00
3	8%	3.46	3.21	2.99	2.54	2.83	2.84
4	26%	3.29	2.92	3.09	2.62	3.68	3.18
5	16%	4.09	3.86	3.68	2.95	4.95	4.43
6	28%	3.73	3.15	3.97	3.08	5.16	4.36
7	8%	3.73	4.89	4.27	3.18	5.23	4.74

Figure 7.1. Finite Mixture Models

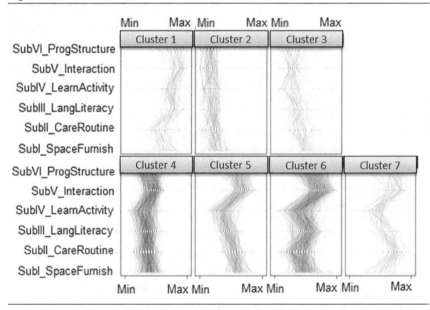

Knowing these patterns of Subscale scores and grouping classrooms together can be useful in designing technical assistance and professional development. It can also identify areas for prioritizing resources for improving quality.

The advantage to this type of analysis is that it allows both policymakers and technical assistance/professional development organizations to target these programs with specific strategies to meet their needs. For instance, during a health emergency such as the Covid-19 pandemic, programs in the groups with low routine care quality could relatively quickly be targeted for special health and hygiene training or strengthened regulatory intervention to track progress in this area.

Of particular concern are groups 2 and 4, where classrooms all are scoring mediocre or low across the different dimensions of quality. There is a legitimate concern about the feasibility of making major improvement in quality in these classrooms without large and continuing investments, or perhaps decisions about whether these programs should continue to operate as they are currently configured. If these programs are to continue to operate, intensive support and training will be necessary as well as regulatory interventions with increased site visits and penalties when compliance with regulations continues to lag.

On the other hand, classrooms in group 1 are of moderately high quality but have some issues with Personal Care Routines. Our colleague Debby Cryer has a saying that "sometimes you have to just take your 1s on some Items to get what you want in other areas of the environment." It appears that group 1 programs may have chosen to deemphasize routine care to focus on the other dimensions of quality. One wonders if these classrooms were able to reset their priorities to address a major health crisis as we faced in the Covid-19 pandemic and to protect children from harm. Group 3 classrooms may have already done something like this. They clearly place a high value on routine care while being able to maintain relatively higher scores on Interactions, Program Structure, and even Language and Literacy, although that group's scores on Learning Activities are relatively low.

Groups 5, 6, and 7 all show substantial variation in quality across the ECERS-3 factors. All have strengths as well as weaknesses. There is much to build on with these programs, but targeted efforts on Learning Activities would be a good place to start with classrooms in all three of the clusters.

CHAPTER 8

Special Issues

As the ECERS has become widely used in the United States and beyond, questions have been raised about the applicability of the tool for various populations and in specific settings. As a measure of global quality designed to capture the experiences of children, the tool has been shown to be valid and reliable across multiple studies in the United States (Bisceglia et al., 2009; Burchinal et al., 2011; Burchinal et al., 2002; Burchinal et al., 2006; Cryer et al., 1999; Gordon et al., 2013; Harms et al., 2005; Helburn, 1995; Henry et al., 2004; Hong et al., 2015; Iruka & Morgan, 2014; La Paro et al., 2014; Love et al., 2004; Peisner-Feinberg et al., 1999; Ruzek et al., 2014; Setodji et al., 2013; Whitebook et al., 1989) and in several other countries (Aboud & Hossain, 2011; Bull et al., 2017; Côté et al., 2013; Deynoot-Schaub & Riksen-Walraven, 2006; Goelman et al., 2006; Herrera et al., 2005; Pinto et al., 2013; Sheridan & Schuster, 2001; Sheridan et al., 2009; Sylva et al., 2004; Tietze et al., 1996; Vermeer et al., 2016). However, we also recognize that the tool was written from a particular perspective, and that there may be differences in how well it captures children's experiences depending on context. In this chapter, we consider several issues related to quality measurement for different populations.

USE IN QUALITY RATING AND IMPROVEMENT SYSTEMS AND OTHER HIGH-STAKES APPLICATIONS

Use of observational instruments in high stakes such as state QRIS efforts requires high levels of reliability. In such situations there are significant financial implications for programs because ratings are often used to determine government reimbursement rates for children from low- and moderate-income families. In some states the rates for the highest-rated programs can be as much at 40% higher than for the lowest-rated programs. As a result, many states have provisions for programs to appeal determinations of the ratings. If observation-based assessments cannot be duplicated with accuracy, the systems are not fundamentally sound, and appeal cases will identify such deficiencies and call into question the process for determining reimbursement rates.

ECERS-3 was found to be reliable and valid to the extent possible in the field tests referred to earlier in this book and elsewhere (Harms et al., 2015, pp. 2–5). Following are the results of tests of reliability:

> **Indicator Reliability.** Tests of interrater agreement at the indicator level resulted in a mean reliability of 88.7%.
>
> **Item Reliability.** Mean Item reliability within 1 point was 91%.
>
> **Subscale Reliability.** Mean reliability within 1 point for Subscales ranged from 88% for Program Structure to 100% for Learning Activities.
>
> **Subscale and Total Score.** The Intraclass Correlations of Subscales ranged from .93 to .98 and the total score ICC was .95, indicating acceptable levels of reliability. A more conservative statistic for testing reliability, Cohen's Kappa, considers the magnitude of the differences in scores between observers. The Kappa value obtained in this analysis found an acceptable level of .54 across all scores. It should be noted that Cohen's Kappa is particularly sensitive to extremely low scores, which was the case for several Items in the field test conducted for the measure. Therefore, we might expect the Kappa to be a low estimate of reliability for this sample.

Finally, the field test study examined the internal consistency of scores. Cronbach's Alpha is a measure of the degree to which Items within a Subscale score similarly. Alpha for the full scale score is the degree to which all items in the Scale score together. Alphas for Subscales ranged from .87 to .96 with a full-scale score of .93, indicating that there appears to be a single overall concept being measured by the Total Score and that the Subscales are measuring specific parts of that single concept.

It should be mentioned that after the completion of the field test, some edits were made prior to final publication of ECERS-3. These edits were designed to improve both reliability and consistency. The first full examination of the final, published version of ECERS-3 in a larger and geographically diverse sample in the United States was conducted by Diane Early and colleagues (Early et al., 2018). This study provides evidence that ECERS-3, with appropriate training and oversight, is reliable at the total score level. Reliability scores for the state anchors averaged 96%, with no anchor below 91%. Individual data collectors' reliability with their state anchors all met the criteria of 85% reliability within 1 point. In addition, 86 paired observations across the three states found an average 91% agreement within 1 point of the consensus score (Early et al., 2018, p. 345).

The positive findings regarding reliability in both the field test and the Early and colleagues validation study (referred to above) are strong indications that the ECERS-3 can be used successfully in high-stakes situations. However, we have noted an unintended consequence of use in such situations, what we and others have termed "quality for a day." The pressures associated with high-stakes use of the scales have led to staff, often program leaders, taking steps to artificially inflate scores in a classroom on the day of an observation. This has been achieved, for example, by moving extra materials into rooms or moving children out of rooms, either to reduce class sizes or to exclude from classrooms children who are deemed to have challenging behaviors. Others have moved their best teacher into the room being observed just for the day of the observation. We have also heard anecdotally of teacher pay being tied to ECERS scores. The authors of the scale strongly condemn these practices. Such practices are antithetical to efforts to use the scales to build a system of care that supports children and families. Many states and cities have methods to reduce the possibility of such practices. For example, many states provide limited information as to the exact day observations will take place, or they do not select the classroom(s) to be observed until the observers arrive. They also train observers to watch for children being removed from the observation room or for a change in teachers. In general, those in charge of the assessments should be aware of such possibilities and, depending on how programs might be trying to inflate scores artificially, seek methods to reduce the possibility of such cheating.

There is a misconception among some that the goal for a classroom would be to achieve a score of 7 on every Item of the ECERS. The way the ECERS was constructed makes this a virtual impossibility. The ECERS Items are designed to measure a range of quality factors across a range of quality levels. It is expected that every classroom has strengths and weaknesses, and they will not be "perfect" across all areas. To accomplish this, it is necessary for observers to be carefully trained to score exactly what is seen during the observation and not rely on something a teacher might say to them or to "guess" what they think would happen in various situations. Designing the scale in this way allows a primary purpose of the tool to guide continuous quality improvement.

RACE, ETHNICITY, AND EQUITY

The ECERS was written by a team of early childhood professionals with expertise in early childhood settings, child development, early childhood curricula, and measurement. Together, the team has decades of experience as teachers and directors/principals of early childhood programs, developers of curricula, providers of training/technical assistance, and researchers in early childhood settings. The experience and expertise brought by the author team qualifies them well to develop measurement tools and has enabled them to create a set of measures that have transformed the field. Nevertheless, the author team brings a set of perspectives that represent their cultural values. Given recent national conversations about racial equity, all of the methods and processes used in the early childhood field warrant scrutiny to ensure that they are free from bias and promote equitable outcomes. As described in Chapter 9, "Future Work," the authors are working on detailed analyses of existing data and will conduct more targeted research on issues of diversity as part of the preparation for the next generation of ERS instruments. There is much to be done in this area.

The ECERS has been used widely by observers of various races/ethnicities, in classrooms taught by teachers of various races, and in environments serving children of various races. Many of the large-scale studies of early childhood that have used the various editions of ECERS have included primarily children from families living in poverty, which in the United States disproportionately represent children and families of color. The current available evidence suggests that the ECERS demonstrates comparable high levels of reliability and validity for White, Black, and Latinx children (Burchinal & Cryer, 2003), indicating that the ECERS is valid and reliable for diverse populations. In addition, in a separate article, Burchinal and colleagues (2000) found limited support for quality being related to children's development for all children, and quite limited support that child care quality matters more for children experiencing social risk factors. They also found that quality of care is more important for language development for children of color than for White non-Hispanic children.

During the revision process in developing ECERS-3, the authors convened a focus group of professionals who had experience working with diverse populations and who were involved in the use of ECERS-R in such settings. This focus group rejected the idea of having a set of separate Items in a revised edition, indicating that the attention to serving diverse populations of children should not be relegated to just a few Items. The issues cut across all aspects of early childhood environments. The group urged modification of individual Items and Indicators to identify issues more clearly in serving these populations. Changes were made to expand attention to these issues, but no specific research has been conducted to examine the degree to which the ECERS-3 fully addresses the fundamental issues in providing inclusive environments for children living in a diverse society. The additional studies of the ECERS-3 mentioned above are needed to distinguish between White-majority, Black-majority, Latinx-majority, and diverse classrooms to illuminate possible differences in the quality of experiences of children. In addition, more detailed examinations of racial-ethnic match between children and staff and between staff and ECERS observers may be revealing. Finally, next revisions of the ERS tools would benefit from extensive review by a team of experts that represent diverse racial, ethnic, and cultural backgrounds or the inclusion of authors who expand the cultural perspectives of the tools.

SERVING CHILDREN WITH DISABILITIES

As with the issue of diverse populations described above, there are concerns about any relationship between the quality of classrooms and the presence/absence of children with special needs. In making revisions for ECERS-3, the authors convened a focus group of teachers and special educators to address the need and means of measuring the quality of settings for children with special needs. The recommendations from the focus group were quite similar to those from the focus group on diverse populations. That is, they downplayed the need for additional Items or for a new Subscale, indicating that providing high quality for children with special needs cut across the full spectrum of quality represented in the ECERS. Any needs beyond that should be dealt with in a separate instrument. Other researchers have been working on such measures (Soukakou, 2012).

In a study using the original ECERS, Bailey and colleagues (1982) found that children in self-contained special education preschool classrooms had large amounts of time when they were not engaged in any productive activities but were waiting for a therapist or other special educator to teach them. These classrooms scored lower on Learning Activities than classrooms with typical child care programs. While the situation has changed in both child care and special education classrooms since that time, this study does point to concerns for how children with special needs are served in both self-contained and inclusive preschool classrooms.

Some agencies have found that the ECERS instruments are valuable in identifying promising classrooms for becoming inclusive settings for children with special needs (Thelma Harms, personal communication).

NATIONAL NORMS

There are no truly national norms for ECERS scores for either ECERS-R or ECERS-3. The United States does not have a real system of services, but rather a patchwork of mostly small programs operated largely independent of one another (although this is changing). Early care and education services are offered in a wide variety of settings and programs, each with its own strengths and weaknesses. A study comparing ECERS scores in the United States with those in four European Countries—Germany, Austria, Spain, and Portugal—found that early childhood services in the European countries that had national standards and heavy government involvement were more uniform than services in the U.S. sample. In the U.S. context there were more very-high- and very-low-quality programs than in the European countries even though the average quality was not significantly different for the United States compared to the European counterparts (Cryer et al., 1999). The NCEDL study of state-funded Pre-K programs (Clifford et al., 2005) found less variation in quality, more in line with what was found in the earlier study, although the overall average of scores was lower than expected. The moderate level of quality may be in part because the study was done when Pre-K programs were relatively new in the states where the study took place.

For studies using the ECERS-R, probably the best nationwide picture is given by the Early Childhood Longitudinal Study, Birth Cohort (ECLS-B). This was a study of children born in 2001; the child care observations were done in 2005–2006. The study sample was 750 children whose families were eligible for child care subsidies. The total score for the 750 classrooms/homes these children were in was 4.06 (includes both center-based classrooms and family child care homes). Centers averaged 4.48 for classrooms with children receiving subsidies and 4.19 for classrooms for those serving the children who were not receiving subsidies. Scores for Head Start classrooms averaged 4.54, and public Pre-K classrooms averaged 4.75. All assessments were done by assessors trained to reliability, and all were fully independent of the programs being observed. Even in this well-designed and well-executed study, the results are not reflective of the totality of preschool classrooms in the United States, so comparisons must be made with caution. Also, this study used a truncated version of the ECERS-R, which further limits comparisons with other studies (Johnson et al., 2012).

Studies of Head Start, State QRIS efforts, or Pre-K systems often seek to get normative data for their own purposes. If studies have well trained and monitored data collectors who are using standardized procedures, it is possible to obtain meaningful results. Sometimes such studies do not use all of the Items in the scale, or they develop their own rules for scoring (i.e., they alter the scoring requirements in the ECERS itself—even if these are seen as simple changes—especially in state QRIS assessments where states may need to adjust scoring to match state early childhood regulations for internal comparison purposes). In such cases, it is appropriate to make comparisons within the specific population of programs being studied, but comparisons beyond that population should be viewed with scrutiny.

The Head Start FACES studies have provided substantial evidence that Head Start programs, on average, score higher on ECERS than other early childhood programs, with average scores reported for preschool Head Start classes somewhat above 5.0 (Aikens et al., 2016; Resnick, 2010; Resnick & Zill, 2002). These data are unique to Head Start and reflect recent efforts to improve quality though requiring staff to have higher levels of education and more in-service training, and resources to purchase materials and equipment and provide higher teacher salaries and benefits.

Finally, the National Center for Early Development and Learning conducted a pair of studies of state-funded Pre-K classrooms in 11 states in 2001–2004 (Early et al., 2005). The studies examined the impact of Pre-K on children who would be entering kindergarten the following year, so had mostly 4-year-olds and some 3-year-olds. Most

(54%) classes were open for less than or equal to 5 hours per day, and the remaining 46% were open more than 5 hours per day. About half of the programs were in schools and the other half in private settings, both for-profit and nonprofit, including Head Start. The Parents/Staff Subscale was not used in these studies. The overall average ECERS-R was 3.80 for the roughly 700 classrooms. In addition to the overall score, factor analysis of the ECERS-R yielded two factors. Factor 1, labeled Teaching and Interactions, is a composite of several indicators including staff–child interactions, discipline, supervision, encouraging children to communicate, and using language to develop reasoning skills. The mean across classrooms on this factor was 4.67 (95% confidence interval: 4.54 to 4.80). The second factor, termed Provisions for Learning, is a composite of indicators such as furnishings, room arrangement, gross motor equipment, art, blocks, dramatic play, and nature/science. The mean across classrooms on this factor was 3.73 (95% confidence interval: 3.63 to 3.82).

It should be noted that all the data in the above studies were using ECERS-R scores. No national-level studies using ECERS-3 have been reported at this time. However, see the tables and figures in Chapter 3 (e.g., Figure 3.3) for data gathered for the ECERS-3 validation study, representing a moderately large sample from three states. Also see the Comparability section in Chapter 2 for advice on comparing ECERS-R and ECERS-3 scores.

INTERNATIONAL USES

As can be seen from the discussions above, the ECERS has been used widely in the world. Currently, there are more than 10 official translations of the ECERS published in various countries from China and Japan in the East, to countries in both North and South America, and in both Western and Eastern Europe, including Russia and the Ukraine. There is one official publication in Arabic. Less formal translations have been done for use in research in many other countries, including studies by international organizations in less well-developed areas in Asia, the Americas, and Africa. The official translations have gone through rigorous testing in the respective countries and have had their content checked though back translation of some type. They are used for specific studies, in professional development and training, and in program self-assessments.

SAFE AND HEALTHY ENVIRONMENTS

From its inception, ECERS was intended to look at environmental support across all of the major areas of children's development, including the impact of early learning environments on child illness and safety.

The Covid-19 pandemic has both highlighted the importance of health concerns in early childhood settings and at the same time made measures of safe and healthy practices in these settings particularly difficult to administer. In general, measurements of these aspects of quality in child care and early education are not well-researched and have not been a central part of the discussion about the impact of quality on children's development. Past studies have focused particularly on spread of infectious disease, especially those spread through contamination of surfaces and through direct contact, and the efficacy of handwashing as a primary prevention method. The authors have been involved in studies with Professor Jonathan Kotch of the UNC-Chapel Hill Gillings School of Global Public Health where we have looked at the impact of environmental issues and illness rates as well as more basic issues related to contamination in early childhood settings (Kotch et al., 1994) and safety issues (Kotch et al., 1993). The emphasis on handwashing in various aspects of care, during routine care, transitions, and generally across the day, is partially built on that work, but also on the work of the American Academy of Pediatrics, the National Public Health Association, and the National Resource Center for Health and Center for Health in Child Care in Denver. Much more in-depth study of the details of disease transmission in early childhood programs is needed.

CHAPTER 9

Future Work

The goal of fully understanding the nature and role of early learning environments in influencing the development of preschool-age children is never ending. Much progress has occurred in understanding the construct of classroom quality and the measurement of that construct in recent years, but we are poised to make even greater gains in understanding how we can design and operate preschool classrooms to the benefit of all children. This chapter provides a discussion of areas for future exploration and development, with the knowledge that there may well be other critical avenues of work. It is our hope that other researchers and practitioners will pick up these threads and other directions toward more precision in our understanding of how best to support children and families through early childhood classroom programming.

EXPLORING ALTERNATIVE STRUCTURES IN THE ECERS-3

As presented in Chapter 3, Item-level data have been used to examine the factor structure of the ECERS-3. Work to replicate the structures found with the data set used in this manual would be helpful. In addition, more work should be conducted with the indicators that comprise the Items to illuminate other possible data structures and scoring mechanisms. For example, Sideris, Clifford, and Neitzel (see Clifford, 2015; Sideris et al., 2014) investigated the possibility of a novel approach to scoring ECERS-R. Their work is based on the understanding that a given Item may relate to multiple factors and that examining the indicators within Items may be a more appropriate method of identifying underlying ways of conceptualizing quality in early learning environments. For instance, Item 10, Meals/Snacks, has indicators related to the nutritional requirements of the meal, the social atmosphere during meals/snacks, and the learning opportunities during meals/snacks, and yet the Item is assigned to only one Subscale and factor in the Item-level factor analyses reported in previous chapters of this book. In addition, in the standard scoring method for ECERS-R, only the indicators needed to determine an Item score must be scored. This leads to a loss of information from indicators at the upper end of the continuum of quality. It should be noted that ECERS-3 has dealt with this issue to some extent by requiring that all indicators be scored regardless of the score for each Item, but the Item score is still dependent only on the indicators up to the point that a score is determined.

In the modified scoring model, the authors of the ECERS-R were asked to identify a full set of possible factors that underlie the concept of quality as expressed in the ERS work. Then each indicator was assigned up to three factors depending on the content of the indicator. All indicators in the ECERS-R (first six Subscales only) are scored regardless of the individual Item scores. Using this revised scoring procedure, confirmatory factor analysis is done at the indicator level to test the fit of the indicators to the newly hypothesized factors.

Using a large sample of some 8,500 assessments from multiple states and types of preschool programs, the hypothesized factors were tested. Of the 22 hypothesized factors, 16 were confirmed, resulting in the option of providing 16 factor scores plus a new total score based on the full set of indicators in the ECERS-R. Factor scores were calculated as the sum of indicator scores for the indicators in a given factor divided by the number of indicators in the factor. The new total score is calculated by summing the indicator scores for all indicators in the scale and then dividing that number by the total number of indicators scored. Preliminary tests of the predictive power of these new scores were performed on a very limited portion of the full sample, which had measures of changes in development over a specified time in classrooms. While very preliminary, the findings tend to support the notion that such a novel approach to scoring could improve the predictive power of the ECERS-R. Similar analyses for the ECERS-3 would be helpful when a large database of scores is accumulated. In addition, new analytic tools, such as machine learning, have emerged from other fields that could be used to further explore the underlying construct of quality.

ENSURING ADEQUATE CONSIDERATION OF EQUITY AND DIVERSITY IN EARLY CHILDHOOD ENVIRONMENTS

As discussed elsewhere in this guide, issues related to the diversity of children and staff are dealt with to some extent in the ECERS-3.

Specific indicators throughout the scale explore efforts to make programs sensitive to the full range of needs of children regardless of race, ethnicity, gender identity, country of origin, or ability. However, the vastly increased recognition of the importance of fully addressing the needs of the diverse population of both children and staff calls for a rethinking of how these diverse needs are addressed in early childhood programs.

Previous studies have found that quality as measured by ECERS (various editions) is more impactful on children of color and children from impoverished backgrounds than for middle-class White children (Burchinal & Cryer, 2003). Similarly, studies have shown that children with special needs sometimes encounter more supportive environments in typical child care than in self-contained classes (Bailey et al., 1982). Studies are needed to further explore these relationships. Future editions of the ECERS will also need to address issues for these populations in more detail.

FOCUSING ON SPECIFIC FEATURES OF PROGRAMMING: EXTENSIONS OF THE ECERS-3

The ERS authors have been working with a group of researchers and faculty members from other countries regarding extensions of the ERS instruments to focus on specific features of early childhood environments that are particularly important to their own contexts and settings. The first such effort was made by Sylva, Siraj, and Taggart (2010), focusing specifically on four curricular-related areas of keen interest in Britain: *ECERS-E: The Four Curricular Subscales Extension to the Early Childhood Environment Rating Scale (ECERS-R) with Planning Notes*, 4th edition. Developed to fit with national expectations and exams, the instrument has been successfully employed in major studies in the United Kingdom.

More recently, a team of researchers from Moscow City University (Yakshina et al., 2021) has been working on a scale extension specifically focusing on play from a Vygotskyan point of view. This same team is also looking at provisions for the development of creativity in children as another extension of ECERS. It is expected that the ERS authors will continue to collaborate with these and similar groups and encourage such efforts.

EXPANDING INTERNATIONAL USE

As noted in the previous chapter, the ECERS has been translated into multiple languages and used around the world. However, most of the translations and usage are in Western countries. In particular, we are unaware of any versions used on the African continent. This represents an area of potential expansion. By bringing the scales to new cultures, we can expand our conceptions of quality through additional cross-cultural exchanges.

MEASURING ASSOCIATIONS WITH CHILDREN'S OUTCOMES

Finally, more studies are needed examining associations between ECERS-3 quality scores and children's outcomes across a range of developmental areas. A large validation study, from which the data in this guide were drawn, found small correlations between ECERS-3 quality scores and a measure of children's executive functioning (Early et al., 2018). Other studies of the ECERS-3 would be helpful, with cross-cultural samples of children and using a wide battery of outcome measures to understand how quality as measured by the ECERS supports children's learning and development.

CHAPTER 10

Conclusions

In this book, we have tried to look at a full range of issues in understanding what quality means in early childhood classrooms, and factors that are associated with quality toward an understanding of how quality can be improved. We began by looking at the situation in society that has led to the explosion in nonparental early care and education, particularly in the United States. The goal was to gain further understanding of how we got here to give us perspective in how changes in our society might affect early care and education in the future. Fundamental to expected changes is the rapidity with which family life has changed and may change in the next decade or two.

We then turned to defining quality in early care and learning environments: What does quality really mean? How can we measure it in reliable and valid ways? Using a vision of what impacts young children in their early years developed by Urie Bronfenbrenner, we created a theory of change for early care and education that shows that a wide variety of factors affect children's outcomes over their lifetimes, and that we can look at what happens specifically in early learning environments to determine how these environments may affect children. This model also allows for examination of the various factors in the larger environment that affect what happens in early learning environments to facilitate improvement in those environments to enable the provision of high-quality care.

After providing background information on the ECERS, we turned to examples of descriptive analyses that can be used to analyze ECERS data and understand components of quality. Chapter 3 demonstrated how one can report and portray data in easy-to-understand charts and graphs that enable users to spot potential strengths and weaknesses. Using data from a moderately large data set from three states, we provided a variety of methods for examining the distribution of scores and their variability and eventually attempting to understand the factor structure of quality as measured by ECERS-3.

In Chapters 4 through 7, we explored in some detail the relationships between classroom quality and a variety of characteristics of those classrooms. As in previous chapters, the goal was to provide models of analysis that may prove to be useful to program administrators, professional development experts, evaluators, and policymakers. We used increasingly complex statistical tools to look at the fine details of relationships between quality and the different characteristics of classrooms and programs. We also introduced analytic techniques in these chapters (as well as more techniques later in the Appendix) that are less commonly used in educational and psychological research to encourage the field to apply a variety of methods in analyzing and understanding classroom quality data. Such analyses can be powerful tools in guiding policies at the individual program level and particularly at regional, state, and even federal levels.

Chapter 8 presented a discussion of six major issues that arise in the use of ECERS-3 in different circumstances for particular purposes. As in previous chapters, the intent was to provide a background and examination of critical elements in providing high-quality care and education to all children in nonparental care. We then devoted Chapter 9 to a discussion of future issues and areas to consider in assessing learning environments.

Throughout this book, we used a moderately large data set of classroom observations gathered across three states to show the types of analyses that can be conducted with ECERS-3 data. The primary purpose of these analyses was demonstration, but some interesting findings emerged. We found associations between structural characteristics of classrooms, such as length of day, lead teacher education, and teacher/child ratio, and quality as measured with the ECERS-3. These findings have appeared in previous studies of earlier versions of the ECERS, although teacher education is a characteristic that has been controversial (Early et al., 2007). We also found some potential moderating effects of variables that warrant additional exploration, such as between the proportion of children with disabilities and length of day in association with classroom quality. We also found some potentially interesting relations between structural characteristics and quality that may vary by program types—Head Start versus non–Head Start, pre-K versus non–pre-K, and programs located in elementary schools versus nonschool settings. Many of the relations and interactions have policy implications, as we have highlighted.

Following the Appendix, an extensive bibliography provides both references for citations throughout the book and additional relevant materials for those studying these issues. It is our hope that this book provides critical information for those interested in early learning environments and the impact of these environments on young children.

Supplementary Analyses

The chapters in this guide presented results of analytic methods commonly used in educational and psychological research, including regression models, hierarchical models, and structural equations. This Appendix presents three additional sections. The first offers results of an analytic method that is less commonly used in educational research but is widely used in other fields, including econometrics and sociology. The second presents a description of Rasch modeling techniques to understand whether for some ECERS-3 quality Items it is easier or more difficult to achieve higher scores. The third demonstrates the value of differential item functioning (DIF) in examining whether items function differently for different types of programs. These more complex analyses are presented to introduce readers to these methods and to encourage use of varied methods in data analyses to better understand early education quality and its associations with inputs, outputs, and outcomes.

BLINDER-OAXACA DECOMPOSITION

The decomposition method (Blinder, 1973; Jann, 2008; Oaxaca, 1973; Oaxaca & Ransom, 1994) allows the decomposition of differences in mean outcomes between two groups into a part that is due to differences in observed characteristics and a part that is due to differences in the estimated coefficients. In the context of a linear regression, the mean outcome for Group $G \in \{A, B\}$ can be expressed as $\bar{Y}_G = \bar{X}'_G \hat{\beta}_G$, in which $\bar{X}'_G$ contains the mean values of independent variables and $\hat{\beta}_G$ contains the estimated coefficients. Therefore, $\Delta \bar{Y}$ can be rewritten as:

$$\Delta \bar{Y} = \bar{X}'_A \hat{\beta}_A - \bar{X}'_B \hat{\beta}_B$$

In turn, this can be expressed as the sum of the following three terms:

$$\Delta \bar{Y} = \underbrace{\left(\bar{X}_A - \bar{X}_B\right)' \hat{\beta}_B}_{endowments} + \underbrace{\bar{X}_B'\left(\hat{\beta}_A - \hat{\beta}_B\right)}_{coefficients} + \underbrace{\left(\bar{X}_A - \bar{X}_B\right)'\left(\hat{\beta}_A - \hat{\beta}_B\right)}_{interaction}$$

This method is called the threefold Blinder-Oaxaca decomposition of the mean outcome difference, termed threefold because of the three terms in the above equation. The endowments term refers to the contribution of differences in independent variables between groups. The coefficients term refers to the part that is due to group differences in the coefficients. The interaction term demonstrates that cross-group differences in independent variables and coefficients can occur at the same time.

For example, the mean ECERS-3 score for classrooms not located in elementary schools is 3.59 (Group A), and the mean score is 3.66 for classrooms physically located in elementary schools (Group B), leaving the difference of approximately −0.07 to be explained by the Blinder-Oaxaca decomposition (i.e., classrooms in schools tend to have higher-quality scores than classrooms not located at schools). To understand what is driving this difference, we can examine its component parts. The results of the threefold decomposition suggest that, of the −0.07 difference, approximately −0.03 can be attributed to group differences in endowments and −0.01 to differences in coefficients; the remaining −0.03 is accounted for by the interaction of the two.

Figure A.1. The Coefficients Components of a Threefold Blinder-Oaxaca Decomposition of the Group A and B ECERS Scores

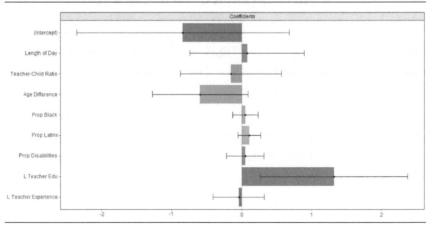

Most variables in the coefficients component are either insignificant or exhibit only marginal statistical significance. The only variable achieving clear statistical significance is lead teacher's educational level. As differences in educational level coefficients between Group A and B show, the association between ECERS-3 scores and educational level is greater for classrooms not physically located at elementary schools by almost 0.36. As Figure A.1 makes clear, differences in regression coefficients on Lead Teacher's Educational Level account for the decisive portion of the difference in the total ECERS-3 score. On the other hand, variables in the endowments component are statistically insignificant.

ITEM RESPONSE THEORY: RASCH MODEL
WITHOUT COVARIATES

We now turn to explicitly lay out the possibilities for item response theory (IRT) modeling with the multilevel modeling function (de Boeck et al., 2011). The model is described for an item response context, with classrooms as groups, items for the repeated observations, and binary responses (i.e., "low" defined as ECERS-3 scores of 1–4 and "high" defined as ECERS-3 scores of 5–7). We created the "low" and "high" quality categories because the use of multilevel modeling for IRT is limited to binary data and ordered-category data that can be decomposed into binary data (Rijmen et al. 2003; Tutz, 1990).

In particular, the Rasch model uses $I+1$ item covariates: I item indicators plus a constant 1 for all items. Consequently, the $I \times (I+1)$ matrix X of item covariates is the concatenation of a 1-vector and an $I \times I$ identity matrix. The 1-vector has a random effect, which is often defined as the ability or latent feature in an IRT model. Also, the effects of the covariates from the identity matrix are fixed, one per item, and this corresponds to the difficulty parameters. The logistic version of the model is known as the Rasch model, or one-parameter logistic (1PL) model. Regarding item predictors and their effects, the model can be expressed as follows:

Level-1 model:

$$Score_{ij} = \beta_{0j} + \beta_{1j} Item1_{ij} + \beta_{2j} Item2_{ij} + \cdots + \beta_{35j} Item35_{ij} + r_{ij}$$

Level-2 model:

$$\beta_{0j} = \gamma_{00} + u_{0j}, \ \beta_{1j} = \gamma_{10}, \ \beta_{2j} = \gamma_{20}, \cdots, \ \beta_{35j} = \gamma_{350}$$

$$e_{ij} \sim N(0, \sigma^2), \ u_{0j} \sim N(0, \tau^2)$$

Figure A.2. Item Difficulties

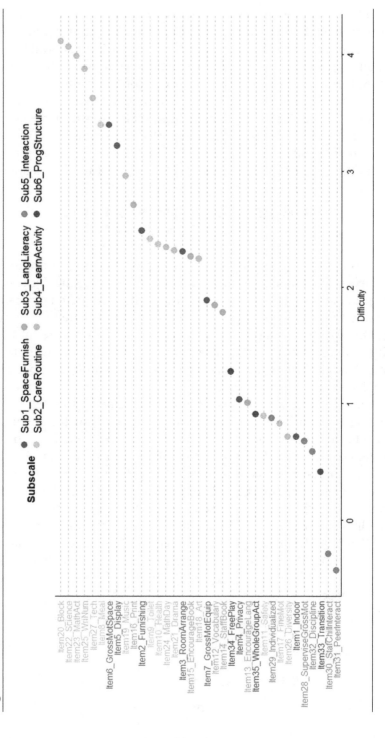

where S*core*$_{ij}$ is the binary outcome variable (0 = "Low" ECERS-3 score of 1–4; 1 = "High" ECERS-3 score of 5–7) for item i in classroom j; *Item*1$_{ij}$, *Item*2$_{ij}$, . . . , *Item*35$_{ij}$ are the binary level-1 variables; γ_{00} is a level-2 coefficient (fixed effects); and γ_{10}, γ_{20}, . . . , γ_{350} are coefficients of the level-2 variables.

In the output, the fixed effects refer to the estimated item (difficulty) parameters for the Items (see Figure A.2). The five most difficult Items were *Blocks, Nature/science, Math materials and activities, Appropriate use of technology,* and *Meals/snacks.* The five easiest Items were *Peer interaction, Staff–child interaction, Transitions and waiting times, Discipline,* and *Supervision of gross motor.* Overall, this indicates that the Items within the *Interaction* Subscale are more likely to have a high score (i.e., ECERS-3 score 5–7) given the classroom's level of the latent trait (i.e., quality).

As can be seen in Figure A.2, the Items are distributed across the difficulty index covering the full range of difficulty. As noted previously, the Items in the Learning Activities Subscale (original Subscale) tend to be difficult for classrooms to achieve. These Items generally require both appropriate materials and appropriate teaching strategies in using the materials. More study at the Indicator level is needed to fully understand the degree to which the teacher involvement results in the difficulty indicated here.

DIFFERENTIAL ITEM FUNCTIONING

One application of this type of analysis is to see whether Items function differently for distinct groups. Differential item functioning (DIF) occurs when respondents from different groups with the same latent ability have different probabilities of endorsing a given Item on a multi-Item scale (Osterlind & Everson, 2009; Thissen et al., 1993). If an Item functions differently for two groups, it is possible that (1) the Item taps a dimension of the latent feature measured in the scale that manifests differently between the groups or (2) there are artifactual elements in the measurement process (e.g., different understanding of a word; Breslau et al., 2008). We explored the possibility of differential Item functioning in the current sample by examining two groups— Head Start classrooms and non–Head Start classrooms.

We found nonuniform DIFs where particular Items advantage (i.e., are easier for) one of the groups at lower ability (i.e., quality) levels, and the other group at higher ability (i.e., quality) levels (see

Figure A.3. Items Showing Non-Uniform DIFs

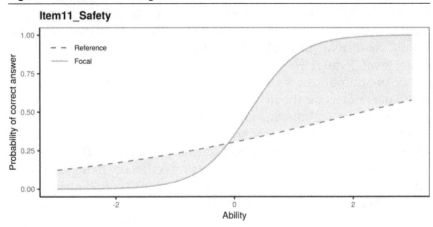

Item11_Safety

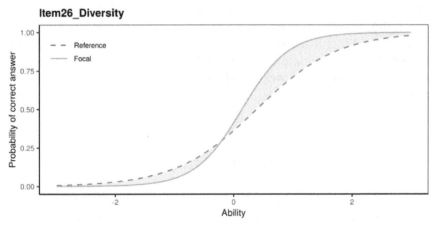

Item26_Diversity

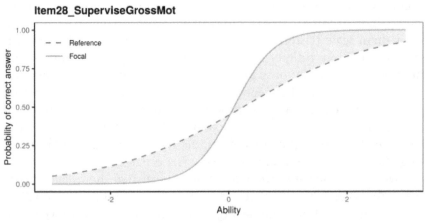

Item28_SuperviseGrossMot

Item30_StafChiIInteract

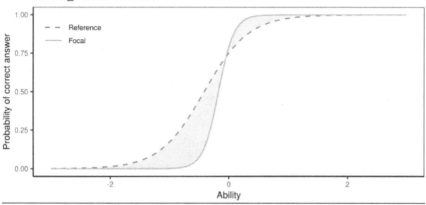

Figure A.3). In this case, the Item has different discrimination (slope) parameters and potentially different difficulty parameters for the two groups. To detect DIFs, we used the Raju test (Raju, 1990) investigating the area between the Item characteristic curves (ICC) of the selected IRT model, fitted separately with data of the two groups. This model employs the 2-parameter logistic (2PL) IRT model. Table A.1 includes information about Raju's Z-statistic and corresponding p-values considering selected adjustment.

As the parameters are estimated separately for the two groups, there is one equation for each group. Parameters a_{iR} and b_{iR} represent discrimination and difficulty for the reference group (for our example, non–Head Start) for Item i. Parameters a_{iF} and b_{iF} represent discrimination and difficulty for the focal group (in our example, Head Start) for Item i.

$$P\left(Y_{pi}=1\mid\theta_p,\ G_p=0\right)=\frac{e^{a_{iR}\left(\theta_p-b_{iR}\right)}}{1+e^{a_{iR}\left(\theta_p-b_{iR}\right)}}$$

$$P\left(Y_{pi}=1\mid\theta_p,\ G_p=1\right)=\frac{e^{a_{iF}\left(\theta_p-b_{iF}\right)}}{1+e^{a_{iF}\left(\theta_p-b_{iF}\right)}}$$

The Raju test showed that four of the 35 Items were indeed exhibiting DIFs. Specifically, the Items *Safety practices, Promoting acceptance of diversity, Supervision of gross motor,* and *Staff-child interactions* gave an advantage to the focal group (i.e., Head Start) at one end of the θ

Table A.1. Raju's Z scores

	Raju's Z
Item 11_Safety	2.08*
Item 26_Diversity	2.03*
Item 28_SuperviseGrossMot	3.11**
Item 30_StafChilInteract	2.80***

** p < 0.001, *** p < 0.01, * p < 0.05

continuum (i.e., latent ability or quality) while favoring the reference group (i.e., non–Head Start) at the other end. Differences in ICCs demonstrate that classrooms from the two groups with identical ability levels (i.e., quality) have unequal probabilities of scoring at high levels (i.e., ECERS-3 score 5–7) on these Items.

These differences are not surprising, since Head Start programs face an additional set of regulations compared to non–Head Start programs, and these differences are likely to have some differential effects on scoring related to the added HS requirements. Overall, the differences are not great.

In designing measures such as the ECERS-3, there is a tension between placing Items that are particularly difficult at the highest level of scoring when they are fundamental to the health, safety, or even intellectual development of children. How can one rate an Item high on a dimension of quality (item) when something very basic, yet easy to provide, is missing? For example, perhaps an observer rates a program overall as good in safety, yet observes staff encouraging some activity that is dangerous to children. This can happen even if other indicators in that Item are rated positively.

A decision to place that indicator on the lower end of the indicators for safety even if it is very hard to achieve is necessary even if indicators above it are easier to rate. So there are tradeoffs between having an Item with the best placement from a statistical standpoint and placing it further down the continuum when the Item is critical for children's development.

Bibliography

Entries preceded by an asterisk are cited in the text.

*Abdi, H. (2003). Factor rotations in factor analysis. In M. Lewis-Beck, A. Bryman, & T. Futing (Eds.), *Encyclopedia of social sciences research methods* (pp. 792–795). Sage.

*Aber, J. L., Tubbs, C., Torrente, C., Halpin, P. F., Johnston, B., Starkey, L., . . . & Wolf, S. (2017). Promoting children's learning and development in conflict-affected countries: Testing change process in the Democratic Republic of the Congo. *Development and Psychopathology, 29*(1), 53–67.

Aboud, F. E. (2006). Evaluation of an early childhood preschool program in rural Bangladesh. *Early Childhood Research Quarterly, 21*, 46–60.

*Aboud, F. E., & Hossain, K. (2011). The impact of preprimary school on primary school achievement in Bangladesh. *Early Childhood Research Quarterly, 26*, 237–246. doi: 10.1016/j.ecresq.2010.07.001

Administration for Children and Families. (2021). *Head Start center location datasets.* https://eclkc.ohs.acf.hhs.gov/policy/45-cfr-chap-xiii

*Afshartous, D., & Preston, R. (2011). Key results of interaction models with centering. *Journal of Statistics Education, 19*(3), 1–24.

*Aikens, N., Bush, C., Gleason, P., Malone, L., & Tarullo, L. (2016). *Tracking quality in Head Start classrooms: FACES 2006 to FACES 2014 technical report.* OPRE Report 2016-95. Office of Planning, Research and Evaluation, Administration for Children and Families, U.S. Department of Health and Human Services, Washington, DC.

American Academy of Pediatrics, American Public Health Association, & National Resource Center for Health and Safety in Child Care. (2002). *Caring for Our Children* (2nd ed.). American Academy of Pediatrics and American Public Health Association.

Andersson, M. (1999). The Early Childhood Environment Rating Scale (ECERS) as a tool in evaluating and improving quality in preschools. *Studies in Educational Sciences, 19*.

*Anders, Y., Rossbach, H., Weinert, S., Ebert, S., Kuger, S., Lehrl, S., & von Maurice, J. (2012). Home and preschool learning environments and their

relations to the development of early numeracy skills. *Early Childhood Research Quarterly, 27*(2), 231–244.

*Arnett, J. (1989). *Caregiver Interaction Scale.* Educational Testing Service.

*Bailey, D. B., Harms, T., & Clifford, R. M. (1982). Comparison of preschool environments for handicapped and non-handicapped children. *Topics in Early Childhood Special Education, 2*(1), 9–20.

Bailey, D. B., Harms, T., & Clifford, R. M. (1983a). Matching changes in preschool environments to desired changes in child behavior. *Journal of Division of Early Childhood, 7,* 61–88.

Bailey, D. B., Harms, T., & Clifford, R. M. (1983b). Social and educational aspects of mealtimes for handicapped preschoolers: Observation and analysis. *Topics in Early Childhood Special Education, 3*(2), 19–32.

Barclay, K., & Benelli, C. (1995). Program evaluation through the eyes of a child. *Childhood Education, 72*(2), 91–97.

Baştürk, R., & Işikğlu, N. (2008). Analyzing process quality of early childhood education with many facet Rasch measurement model. *Educational Sciences: Theory & Practice, 8*(1), 25–32.

Bergen, D. (1995). Quality of the literacy environment in day care and children's development. *Childhood Education, 71*(3), 191–192.

*Berliner, D. C. (1986). In pursuit of the expert pedagogue. *Educational Researcher, 15*(7), 5–13.

*Bisceglia, R., Perlman, M., Schaak, D., & Jenkins, J. (2009). Examining the psychometric properties of the Infant Toddler Environment Rating Scale-Revised Edition in a high stakes context. *Early Childhood Research Quarterly, 24,* 121–132. doi: 10.1016/j.ecresq.2009.02.001

*Blinder, A. S. (1973). Wage discrimination: Reduced form and structural estimates. *Journal of Human Reso*urces, *8*(4), 436–455.

*Bloom, H. S., & Weiland, C. (2015). *Quantifying variation in Head Start effects on young children's cognitive and socio-emotional skills using data from the National Head Start Impact Study.* Available at SSRN 2594430.

*Bowne, J. B., Magnuson, K. A., Schindler, H. S., Duncan, G. J., & Yoshikawa, H. (2017). A meta-analysis of class sizes and ratios in early childhood education programs: Are thresholds of quality associated with greater impacts on cognitive, achievement, and socioemotional outcomes? *Educational Evaluation and Policy Analysis, 39*(3), 407–428.

*Breiman, L. (1995). Better subset regression using the nonnegative garrote. *Technometrics, 37*(4), 373–384.

*Breslau, J., Javaras, K. N., Blacker, D., Murphy, J. M., & Normand, S.L.T. (2008). Differential item functioning between ethnic groups in the epidemiological assessment of depression. *The Journal of Nervous and Mental Disease, 196*(4), 297.

Bronfenbrenner, U. (1979). *The ecology of human development, experiments by nature and design.* Harvard University Press.

Brown, E., Andrews, A. B., & Hutchinson, L. (2008). Bridging the quality gap: Increasing the environmental quality of small independent rural infant-toddler child care. *Early Childhood Services: An Interdisciplinary Journal of Effectiveness, 2*(2), 89–110.

Bryant, D. M., Burchinal, M. R., Lau, L. B., & Sparling, J. J. (1994). Family and classroom correlates of Head Start children's developmental outcomes. *Early Childhood Research Quarterly, 9*(3/4), 289–309.

Bryant, D. M., Clifford, R. M., & Peisner, E. S. (1991). Best practices for beginners: Developmental appropriateness in kindergarten. *American Educational Research Journal, 28*(4), 783–803.

Bryant, D. M., Maxwell, K. L., & Burchinal, M. (1999). Effects of a community initiative on the quality of preschool child care. *Early Childhood Research Quarterly, 14*(4), 449–464.

*Bryant, D., Maxwell, K., Taylor, K., Poe, M., Peisner-Feinberg, E., & Bernier, K. (2003). *Smart Start and preschool child care quality in NC: Change over time and relation to children's readiness.* Chapel Hill, NC: FPG Child Development Institute.

Bryant, D. M., Peisner, E. S., & Clifford, R. M. (1993). *Evaluation of public preschool programs in North Carolina. Final report.* Carolina Policy Studies Program, Frank Porter Graham Child Development Center, University of North Carolina at Chapel Hill.

Buell, M. J., & Cassidy, D. J. (2001). The complex and dynamic nature of quality in early care and educational programs: A case for chaos. *Journal of Research in Childhood Education, 15*(2), 209–220.

*Bull, R., Yao, S-Y, & Ng, E.L. (2017). Assessing quality of kindergarten classrooms in Singapore: Psychometric properties of the Environment Rating Scale—Revised. *International Journal of Early Childhood, 49*(1), 1–20. doi: 10.1007/s13158-017-0180-x

*Burchinal, M. R., & Cryer, D. (2003). Diversity, child care quality, and developmental outcomes. *Early Childhood Research Quarterly, 18*, 401–426. doi: 10.1016/j.ecresq.2003.09.003

*Burchinal, M., Foster, T. J., Bezdek, K. G., Bratsch-Hines, M., Blair, C., & Vernon-Feagans, L. (2020). School-entry skills predicting school-age academic and social–emotional trajectories. *Early Childhood Research Quarterly, 51*, 67–80. doi: 10.1016/j.ecresq.2019.08.004

*Burchinal, M. R., Howes, C., Pianta, R., Bryant, D., Early, D., Clifford, R., & Barbarin, O. (2008). Predicting child outcomes at the end of kindergarten from the quality of pre-kindergarten teacher–child interactions and instruction. *Applied Developmental Science, 12*(3), 140–153.

*Burchinal, M., Kainz, K., & Cai, Y. (2011). How well do our measures of quality predict child outcomes? A meta-analysis of data from large-scale studies of early childhood settings. In M. Zaslow, I. Martinez-Beck, K. Tout, & T. Halle (Eds.), *Quality measurement in early childhood settings* (pp. 11–32). Brookes Publishing Company.

Burchinal, M. R., Peisner-Feinberg, E. S., Bryant, D., & Clifford, R. M. (2000). Children's social and cognitive development and child care quality: Testing for differential associations related to poverty, gender, or ethnicity. *Applied Developmental Science, 4*(3), 149–165.

*Burchinal, M. R., Peisner-Feinberg, E., Pianta, R., & Howes, C. (2002). Development of academic skills from preschool through second grade: Family and classroom predictors of developmental trajectories. *Journal of School Psychology, 40*, 415–436. doi: 10.1016/S0022-4405(02)00107-3

*Burchinal, M. R., Roberts, J. E., Riggins Jr., R., Zeisel, S. A., Neebe, E., & Bryant, D. (2000). Relating quality of center-based child care to early cognitive and language development longitudinally. *Child Development, 71*(2), 339–357.

*Burchinal, M. R., Roberts, J. E., Zeisel, S. A., Hennon, E. A., & Hooper, S. (2006). Social risk and protective child, parenting, and child care factors in early elementary school years. *Parenting: Science and Practice, 6*, 79–113. doi: 10.1207/s15327922par0601_4

Buysse, V., Wesley, P. W., Bryant, D., & Gardner, D. (1999). Quality of early childhood programs in inclusive and noninclusive settings. *Exceptional Children, 65*(3), 301–314.

*Cassidy, D. J., Hestenes, L. L., Hegde, A., Hestenes, S., & Mims, S. (2005). Measurement of quality in preschool child care classrooms: An exploratory and confirmatory factor analysis of the Early Childhood Environment Rating Scale–Revised. *Early Childhood Research Quarterly, 20*, 345–360. doi: 10.1016/j.ecresq.2005.07.005

*Cattell, R. (Ed.). (2012). *The scientific use of factor analysis in behavioral and life sciences.* Springer Science & Business Media.

Clawson, C., & Luze, G. (2008). Individual experiences of children with and without disabilities in early childhood settings. *Topics in Early Childhood Special Education, 28*(3), 132–147.

Clifford, R. M. (1978). The relationship between structure-technology consonance and teacher satisfaction. Dissertation, School of Education, University of North Carolina at Chapel Hill.

Clifford, R. M. (1993). *Recent major studies of early childhood education in the U.S. in Encontro Sobre Educacao Pre-Escolar* (pp. 55–61). Fundacao Calouste Gulbenkian Serviicade Educacao.

Clifford, R. M. (January/April 2013). Estudos em larga escala de educação infantil nos Estados Unidos (Large-scale studies of early childhood education in the United States). *Cad. Pesqui. 43*(148), 98–122.

*Clifford, R. M. (2015, April 14). What's new, what stays the same in the ECERS-3. Presentation to the Educare Learning Network Evaluation Community of Practice.

Clifford, R. M. (November 15, 2015). New ECERS-R virtual subscales: How they benefit you. Presentation at the NAEYC Annual Conference and Expo, Orlando, Florida.

*Clifford, R. M., Barbarin, O., Chang, F., Early, D., Bryant, D., Howes, C., . . . & Pianta, R. (2005). What is pre-kindergarten? Characteristics of public pre-kindergarten programs. *Applied Developmental Science, 9,* 126–143.

Clifford, R. M., Bryant, D. M., & Peisner, E. S. (1989). *Best practices for beginners: Quality programs for kindergartens.* Frank Porter Graham Child Development Center, University of North Carolina at Chapel Hill.

Clifford, R. M., Bryant, D. M., & Peisner, E. S. (1989). Developmental appropriateness of kindergartens in North Carolina. *NC-AEYC News,* North Carolina Association for the Education of Young Children, Raleigh, North Carolina.

Clifford, R. M., Early, D. M., & Hills, T. W. (1999). Almost a million children in school before kindergarten: Who is responsible for early childhood services? *Young Children, 54*(5), 48–51.

Clifford, R. M., Harms, T., & Cryer, D. (1990). Measures of reliability of three rating scales. Paper presented at the annual meeting of the National Association for the Education of Young Children, Washington, DC.

Clifford, R. M., & Rossbach, H-G. (unpublished manuscript). Structure and stability of the Early Childhood Environment Rating Scale. FPG Child Development Institute, Chapel Hill, North Carolina. http://ers.fpg.unc.edu /recent-publications

Clifford, R. M. (2005). Structure and stability of the Early Childhood Environment Rating Scale. In H. Schonfeld, S. O'Brien, & T. Walsh (Eds.), *Questions of quality* (pp. 12–21). The Centre for Early Childhood Development and Education, St. Patrick's College, Dublin, Ireland.

Clifford, R. M., Reszka, S. S., & Rossbach, H. -G. (2010). Reliability and validity of the early childhood environment rating scale. Working paper, Frank Porter Graham Child Development Institute, University of North Carolina at Chapel Hill.

*Clifford, R. M., Yazejian, N., Cryer, D., & Harms, T. (2020). Forty years of measuring quality with the Environment Rating Scales. *Early Childhood Research Quarterly, 51,* 164–166.

Cost, Quality, & Child Outcomes Study Team. (1995a). *Cost, quality, and child outcomes in child care centers: Executive summary.* Economics Department, University of Colorado at Denver.

Cost, Quality, & Child Outcomes Study Team. (1995b). *Cost, quality and child outcomes in child care centers: Public report.* Economics Department, University of Colorado at Denver.

Cost, Quality, & Child Outcomes Study Team. (1995c). *Cost, quality, and child outcomes in child care centers: Key findings and recommendations. Young Children, 50*(4), 40–44.

*Côté, S. M., Mongeau, C., Japel, C., Xu, Q., Séguin, J. R., & Tremblay, R. E. (2013). Child care quality and cognitive development: Trajectories leading to better preacademic skills. *Child Development, 84,* 752–766. doi: 10.1111 /cdev.12007

*Crain, W. (2000). *Theories of development: Concepts and applications*, 4th edition. Prentice Hall.

Cryer, D. (1999). Defining and assessing early childhood program quality. *The Annals of the American Academy of Political and Social Science, 563*, 39–55.

Cryer, D., Clifford, R. M., & Harms, T. (1988). *Day care center compliance and evaluation project: Final report*. Frank Porter Graham Child Development Center, University of North Carolina at Chapel Hill.

Cryer, D., & Phillipsen, L. (1997). Quality details: A close-up look at child care program strengths and weaknesses. *Young Children, 55*(5), 51–61.

*Cryer, D., Tietze, W., Burchinal, M., Leal, T., & Palacios, J. (1999). Predicting process quality from structural quality in preschool programs: A cross-country comparison. *Early Childhood Research Quarterly, 14*, 339–361. doi: 10.1016/S0885-2006(99)00017-4

*De Boeck, P., Bakker, M., Zwitser, R., Nivard, M., Hofman, A., Tuerlinckx, F., & Partchev, I. (2011). The estimation of item response models with the lmer function from the lme4 package in R. *Journal of Statistical Software, 39*(12), 1–28.

*Deming, D. (2009). Early childhood intervention and life-cycle skill development: Evidence from Head Start. *American Economic Journal: Applied Economics, 1*, 111–134.

*Deynoot-Schaub, M.J.G., & Riksen-Walraven, J. M. (2006). Peer contacts of 15-month-olds in childcare: Links with child temperament, parent–child interaction and quality of childcare. *Social Development, 15*, 709–729. doi:10.1111/j.1467-9507.2006.00366.x

Division for Early Childhood Task Force on Recommended Practices. (1993). *DEC recommended practices: Indicators of quality in programs for infants and young children with special needs and their families*. ERIC Document Reproduction Service No. 370–253.

*Early, D., Barbarin, O., Bryant, D., Burchinal, M., Chang, F., Clifford, R., . . . & Barnett, W. S. (2005). *Pre-kindergarten in eleven states: NCEDL's multi-state study of pre-kindergarten & study of State-Wide Early Education Programs (SWEEP): Preliminary descriptive report*. Frank Porter Graham Child Development Institute, Chapel Hill, North Carolina.

*Early, D. M., Bryant, D. M., Pianta, R. C., Clifford, R. M., Burchinal, M. R., Ritchie, S., . . . & Barbarin, O. (2006). Are teachers' education, major, and credentials related to classroom quality and children's academic gains in pre-kindergarten? *Early Childhood Research Quarterly, 21*, 174–195. doi: 10.1016/j.ecresq.2006.04.004

*Early, D. M., Maxwell, K. L., Burchinal, M., Bender, R. H., Ebanks, C., Henry, G. T., Iriondo-Perez, J. . . . & Zill, N. (2007). Teachers' education, classroom quality, and young children's academic skills: Results from seven studies of preschool programs. *Child Development, 78*(2), 558–580.

*Early, D. M., Sideris, J., Neitzel, J., LaForett, D. R., & Nehler, C. G. (2018). Factor structure and validity of the Early Childhood Environment Rating Scale—3rd edition (ECERS-3). *Early Childhood Research Quarterly, 44,* 242–256. doi: 10.1016/j.ecresq.2018.04.009

*Family Development Services. (2021). *Head Start frequently asked questions.* www .fds.org/families/pre-enroll/head-start-frequently-asked-questions

Farquhar, S. (1989). Assessing New Zealand child day care quality using the Early Childhood Environment Rating Scale. *Early Child Development and Care, 47,* 93–105.

File, N. K., & Kontos, S. (1993). The relationship of program quality to children's play in integrated early intervention settings. *Topics in Early Childhood Special Education, 13,* 1–18.

*Frede, E., Jung, K., Barnett, W. S., Lamy, C. E., & Figueras, A. (2007). The Abbott Preschool Program Longitudinal Effects Study (APPLES): Interim report. National Institute for Early Education Research, New Brunswick, New Jersey.

*Friedrich, R. (1982). In defense of multiplicative terms in multiple regression equations. *American Journal of Political Science, 26*(4), 797–833.

Fugimoto, K. A., Gordon, R. A., Feng, F., & Hofer, K. G. (2018). Examining the category functioning of the ECERS-R across eight data sets. *AERA Open, 4*(1), 1–16. doi: 10.1177/2332858418758299

*Gallagher, J. J. (2015). Political issues in gifted education. *Journal for the Education of the Gifted, 38,* 77–89. doi: 10.1177/0162353214565546

*Gesell, A., & Ilg, F. L. (1943). *Infant and child in the culture of today.* Harper Brothers.

Goelman, H. (1988). A study of the relationships between structure and process variables in home and day care settings on children's language development. In A. R. Pence (Ed.), *Ecological research with children and families: From concepts to methodology.* Teachers College Press.

Goelman, H., Forer, B., Kershaw, P., Doherty, G., Lero, D., & LaGrange, A. (2006). Towards a predictive model of quality in Canadian child care centers. *Early Childhood Research Quarterly, 21*(3), 280–295.

Goelman, H., & Pence, A. R. (1987). The relationship between family structure and child development in three types of day care. In S. Kontos & D. Peters (Eds.), *Advances in Applied Developmental Psychology* (Vol. 2, pp. 129–146). Ablex.

Goelman, H., & Pence, A. R. (1988). Children in three types of day care: Daily experiences, quality of care and developmental outcomes. *Early Child Development and Care, 33,* 67–76.

*Goldin, C. D. (1991). The role of World War II in the rise of women's employment. *The American Economic Review, 81,* 741–756.

*Gordon, R. A., Fujimoto, K., Kaestner, R., Korenman, S., & Abner, K. (2013). An assessment of the validity of the ECERS-R with implications for assessments of child care quality and its relation to child development. *Developmental Psychology, 49,* 146–160. doi: 10.1037/a0027899

*Gordon, R. A., Hofer, K. G., Fujimoto, K., Risk, N., Kaestner, R., & Koren-
man, S. (2015). Identifying high-quality preschool programs: New evidence
on the validity of the Early Childhood Environment Rating Scale-Revised
(ECERS-R) in relation to school readiness goals. *Early Education and Development, 26*(8), 1086–1110.

*Gunes, F. (2015). *Penalized regression methods for linear models in SAS/STAT®.*
https://support.sas.com/rnd/app/stat/papers/2015/PenalizedRegression
_LinearModels.pdf

Hagekull, B., & Bohlin, G. (1995). Day care quality, family and child characteristics and socioemotional development. *Early Childhood Research Quarterly, 10*(4), 505–526.

*Hair, F., Hult, M., Ringle, C., & Sarstedt, M. (2016). *A primer on partial least
squares structural equation modeling (PLS-SEM).* Sage.

Harms, T. (2000). Using the environmental rating scales as a catalyst for
change. In C.S.L. Tan-Niam & Q. M. Ling (Eds.), *Investing in our future:
The early years (*pp. 25–35). McGraw-Hill.

*Harms, T., & Clifford, R. M. (1978). *The Day Care Environment Rating Scale.*
Frank Porter Graham Child Development Center, University of North
Carolina at Chapel Hill.

*Harms, T., & Clifford, R. M. (1980). *Early Childhood Environment Rating Scale.*
Teachers College Press.

*Harms, T., & Clifford, R. M. (1989). *Family Day Care Rating Scale.* Teachers
College Press.

Harms, T., & Clifford, R. M. (1993). Studying educational settings. In B. Spodek
(Ed.), *Handbook of research on the education of young children* (pp. 477–492).
Macmillan.

*Harms, T., Clifford, R. M., & Cryer, D. (1998). *Early Childhood Environment
Rating Scale-Revised.* Teachers College Press.

*Harms, T., Clifford, R. M., & Cryer, D. (2005). *Early Childhood Environment
Rating Scale-Revised (Updated).* Teachers College Press.

*Harms, T., Clifford, R. M., & Cryer, D. (2015). *Early Childhood Environment
Rating Scale,* 3rd edition. Teachers College Press.

*Harms, T., Cryer, D., & Clifford, R. M. (1990). *Infant/Toddler Environment Rat-
ing Scale.* Teachers College Press.

Harms, T. H., Rossbach, H. G., & Clifford, R. M. (June 1991). *A theoretical
framework for looking at early childhood environments.* Presented at the National Head Start Conference, Washington, DC.

*Hastie, T., & Tibshirani, R. (1987). Generalized additive models: Some ap-
plications. *Journal of the American Statistical Association, 82*(398), 371–386.

*Hastie, T., Tibshirani, R, & Wainwright, M. (2015). *Statistical Learning with
Sparsity: The Lasso and Generalizations.* Chapman and Hall.

*Helburn, S. (Ed.). (1995). *Cost, quality, and child outcomes in child care centers:
Technical report.* University of Colorado, Department of Economics, Center
for Research in Economic Social Policy.

Helburn, S. W., Culkin, M. L., Morris, J. R., & Clifford, R. M. (1995). *The cost, quality, and child outcomes study theoretical structure.* In S. W. Helburn (Ed.), *Cost, quality and child outcomes in child care centers, technical report.* University of Colorado, Economics Department, University of Colorado at Denver.

*Henry, G. T., Ponder, B., Rickman, D., Mashburn, A., Henderson, L., & Gordon, C. (2004, December). *An evaluation of the implementation of Georgia's pre-K program: Report of the findings from the Georgia Early Childhood Study (2002–03).* Georgia State University, School of Policy Studies, Applied Research Center, Atlanta, Georgia.

*Herrera, M. O., Mathiesen, M. E., Merino, J. M., & Recart, I. (2005). Learning contexts for young children in Chile: Process quality assessment in preschool centres. *International Journal of Early Years Education, 13,* 13–27.

Hestenes, L. L., Kontos, S., & Bryan, Y. (1993). Children's emotional expression in child care centers varying in quality. *Early Childhood Research Quarterly, 8,* 295–307.

*Hestenes, L. L., Rucker, L., Wang, Y. C., Mims, S. U., Hestenes, S. E., & Cassidy, D. J. (2019). A comparison of the ECERS-R and ECERS-3: Different aspects of quality? *Early Education and Development, 30,* 496–510. doi: 10.1080/10409289.2018.1559681

*Hinitz, B. S. (2014). Head Start: A bridge from past to future. *Young Children, 69*(2), 94.

Honeycutt, D. (2009). The relationship of teacher qualifications, quality of care and student achievement outcomes in the Arkansas Better Chance Program. *Dissertation Abstracts International Section A: Humanities and Social Sciences, 69*(12-A), 4623

*Hong, S.L.S., Howes, C., Marcella, J., Zucker, E., & Huang, Y. (2015). Quality rating and improvement systems: Validation of a local implementation in LA County and children's school-readiness. *Early Childhood Research Quarterly, 30*(Part B), 227–240. doi: 10.1016/j.ecresq.2014.05.0

Hooks, L., Scott-Little, C., Marshall, B., & Brown, G. (2006). Accountability for quality: One state's experience in improving practice. *Early Childhood Education Journal, 33*(6), 399–403.

Howes, C., Phillips, D. A., & Whitebook, M. (1992). Thresholds of quality: Implications for the social development of children in center-based child care. *Child Development, 62*(2), 449–460.

*Hu, L. T., & Bentler, P. M. (1999). Cutoff criteria for fit indexes in covariance structure analysis: Conventional criteria versus new alternatives. *Structural Equation Modeling: A Multidisciplinary Journal, 6*(1), 1–55.

Hu, B. Y., & Szente J. (2009). Exploring the quality of early childhood education in China: Implications for early childhood teacher education. *Journal of Early Childhood Teacher Education, 30*(3), 247–262.

Huang, P. H. (2017). Asymptotics of AIC, BIC, and RMSEA for model selection in structural equation modeling. *Psychometrika, 82*(2), 407–426.

*Hulsey, L. K., Aikens, N., Kopack, A., West, J., Moiduddin, E., & Tarullo, L. (2011). *Head Start children, families, and programs: Present and past data from FACES*. OPRE Report 2011–33a. Office of Planning, Research and Evaluation, Administration for Children and Families, U.S. Department of Health and Human Services, Washington, DC.

*Imai, K., Keele, L., Tingley, D., & Yamamoto, T. (2010). Causal mediation analysis using R. In Vinod H. (Eds.), *Advances in social science research using R* (pp. 129–154). Springer.

*Iruka, I. U., & Morgan, J. (2014). Patterns of quality experienced by African American children in early education programs: Predictors and links to children's preschool and kindergarten academic outcomes. *The Journal of Negro Education, 83*, 235–255. doi: 10.7709/jnegroeducation.83.3.0235

Ishimine, K., & Wilson, R. (2009). Centre-based child care quality in urban Australia. *Australasian Journal of Early Childhood, 34*(3), 19–28.

*Jann, B. (2008). The Blinder–Oaxaca decomposition for linear regression models. *The Stata Journal, 8*(4), 453–479.

Jennrich, R. I. (2002). A simple general method for oblique rotation. *Psychometrika, 67*(1), 7–19.

*Johnson, A., Ryan, R., & Brooks-Gunn, J. (2012). Child-care subsidies: Do they impact the quality of care children experience? *Child Development, 83*(4), 1444–1461. http://www.jstor.org/stable/23255704

Kagan, S. L., Clifford, R. M., Helburn, S. W., & The Research Team. (1995). Major findings and recommendations. In S. W. Helburn (Ed.), *Cost, quality and child outcomes in child care centers, technical report*. Department of Economics, University of Colorado at Denver.

*Kammerman, S. B., & Gatenio, S. (2003). Overview of the current policy context. In D. Cryer & R. M. Clifford, *Early Childhood and Care in the USA* (pp. 1–30). Paul H. Brookes.

Karoly, L. A., Ghosh-Dastidar, B., & Zellman, G. L. (2008). *Prepared to learn: The nature and quality of early care and education for preschool-age children in California*. Rand Corporation.

Kärrby, G., & Giota, J. (1994). Dimensions of quality in Swedish day care centers: An analysis of the Early Childhood Environment Rating Scale. *Early Child Development and Care, 104*, 1–22.

Kärrby, G., & Giota, J. (1995). Parental conceptions of quality in daycare centers in relation to quality measured by the ECERS. *Early Child Development and Care, 110*(95), 1–18.

Kontos, S., & Fiene, R. (1987). *Child care quality, compliance with regulations, and children's development: The Pennsylvania study*. National Association for the Education of Young Children.

Kotch, J., Loda, F., Harms, T., Clifford, R., & McMurray, M. P. (1993). Parents' reports of home and out-of-home injuries among children attending child care centers. *Early Child Development and Care, 96*, 183–193.

Kotch, J. B., Weigle, K. A., Weber, D. J., Clifford, R. M., Harms, T., Loda, F. A., . . . & Faircloth, A. H. (1994). Evaluation of hygienic intervention in child day-care centers. *Pediatrics, 94*(6), 991–994.

Kwan, C., Sylva, K., & Reeves, B. (1988). Day care quality and child development in Singapore. *Early Child Development and Care, 144*, 69–77.

*La Paro, K. M., Williamson, A. C., & Hatfield, B. (2014). Assessing quality in toddler classrooms using the CLASS-Toddler and the ITERS-R. *Early Education and Development, 25*, 875–893. doi: 10.1080/10409289.2014.883586

Lera, M. J. (1996). Education under five in Spain: A study of preschool classes in Seville. *European Journal of Psychology of Education, 11*(2), 139–150.

Lera, M. J., Owen, C., & Moss, P. (2007). Quality of educational settings for four-year-old children in England. *European Early Childhood Education Research Journal, 4*(2), 21–32.

Loeb, S., Fuller, B., Kagan, S. L., & Carrol, B. (2004). Child care in poor communities: Early learning effects of type, quality, and stability. *Child Development, 75*(1), 47–65.

*LoCasale-Crouch, J., Konold, T., Pianta, R., Howes, C., Burchinal, M., Bryant, D., . . . & Barbarin, O. (2007). Observed classroom quality profiles in state-funded pre-kindergarten programs and associations with teacher, program, and classroom characteristics. *Early Childhood Research Quarterly, 22*(1), 3–17.

*Love, J. M., Constantine, J., Paulsell, D., Boller, K., Ross, C., Raikes, H., . . . & Brooks-Gunn, J. (2004). The role of Early Head Start programs in addressing the child care needs of low-income families with infants and toddlers: Influences on child care use and quality. U.S. Department of Health and Human Services.

*Ludwig, J., & Miller, D. L. (2007). Does Head Start improve children's life chances: Evidence from a regression discontinuity design. *Quarterly Journal of Economics, 122*, 159—208.

Luis, A. (2009). Preschool education in Belize: Research on the current status and implications for the future. *Dissertation Abstracts International Section A: Humanities and Social Sciences, 69*(7-A), 2593.

Lyon, M. E., & Canning, P. M. (1997). Auspice, location, provincial legislation and funding of day care in Atlantic Canada: Relationships with centre quality and implications for policy. *Canadian Journal of Research in Early Childhood Education, 6*(2), 139–155.

*Manning, M., Garvis, S., Fleming, C., & Wong, G.T.W. (2017). The relationship between teacher qualification and the quality of the early childhood care and learning environment. *Campbell Systematic Reviews* (2017), 1. doi: 10.4073/csr.2017.1

*Mashburn, A. J., Pianta, R. C., Hamre, B. K., Downer, J. T., Barbarin, O. A., Bryant, D., . . . & Howes, C. (2008). Measures of classroom quality in prekindergarten and children's development of academic, language, and social skills. *Child Development, 79*(3), 732–749.

Mathers, S., Linskey, F., Seddon, J., & Sylva, K. (2007). Using quality rating scales for professional development: Experiences from the UK. *International Journal of Early Years Education, 15,* 261–274. doi: 10.1080/09669760701516959

Maxwell, K., & Bryant, D. (1996). *Overall summary of Smart Start Evaluation 1994–95 Child Care Data.* Frank Porter Graham Child Development Center, University of North Carolina at Chapel Hill.

*Maxwell, K. L., Early, D. M., Bryant, D., Kraus, S., Hume, K., & Crawford, G. (2009). *Georgia study of early care and education: Findings from Georgia's Pre-K Program.* University of North Carolina, FPG Child Development Institute.

*Mayer, D., & Beckh, K. (2016). Examining the validity of the ECERS–R: Results from the German National Study of Child Care in Early Childhood. *Early Childhood Research Quarterly, 36,* 415–426. doi: 10.1016/j.ecresq.2016.01.001

McCartney, K. (1984). Effects of quality of day care environment on children's language development. *Developmental Psychology, 20*(2).

McCartney, K., Scarr, S., Phillips, D., & Grajek, S. (1985). Day care as intervention: Comparisons of quality day care programs. *Journal of Applied Developmental Psychology, 6(*3), 247–260.

*McWayne, C. M., Green, L. E., & Fantuzzo, J. W. (2009). A variable- and person-oriented investigation of preschool competencies and Head Start children's transition to kindergarten and first grade. *Applied Developmental Science, 13*(1), 1–15.

*Melnykov, V., & Maitra, R. (2010). Finite mixture models and model-based clustering. *Statistics Surveys, 4,* 80–116.

*Montes, G., Hightower, A. D., Brugger, L., & Moustafa, E. (2005). Quality child care and socio-emotional risk factors: No evidence of diminishing returns for urban children. *Early Childhood Research Quarterly, 20*(3), 361–372.

*Mulligan, G. M., & Flanagan, K. D. (2006). *Age 2: Findings from the 2-year-old follow-up of the Early Childhood Longitudinal Study, Birth Cohort (ECLS-B)* (NCES 2006-043). U.S. Department of Education & National Center for Education Statistics.

Munton, A. G., Rowland, L., Mooney, A., & Lera, M. J. (1997). Using the Early Childhood Environment Rating Scale (ECERS) to evaluate quality of nursery provision in England: Some data concerning reliability. *Educational Research, 39,* 99–104.

*Neitzel, J., Early, D., Sideris, J., LaForett, D., Abel, M. B., Soli, M., . . . & Wood, J. K. (2019). A comparative analysis of the Early Childhood Environment Rating Scale-Revised and Early Childhood Environment Rating Scale, 3rd edition. *Journal of Early Childhood Research, 17,* 408–422. doi: 10.1177/1476718X19873015

*NICHD Early Child Care Research Network. (2002). Early child care and children's development prior to school entry: Results from the NICHD Study of Early Child Care. *American Educational Research Journal, 39,* 133–164.

*Oaxaca, R. (1973). Male-female wage differentials in urban labor markets. *International Economic Review, 14*(3), 693–709.

*Oaxaca, R. L., & Ransom, M. R. (1994). On discrimination and the decomposition of wage differentials. *Journal of Econometrics, 61*(1), 5–21.

*Organisation for Economic Co-operation and Development (OECD). (2017). Starting strong 2017: Key OECD indicators on early childhood education and care. OECD. http://dx.doi.org/10.1787/9789264276116-3-en

*Osterlind, S. J., & Everson, H. T. (2009). *Differential item functioning*. Sage.

Palacios, J., Lera, M. J., & Moreno, C. (1994). Evaluación de los contextos familiares y extrafamiliares en los años preescolares: Escalas HOME y ECERS (Assessment of family and extrafamily contexts during the preschool years: HOME and ECERS Scales). *Infancia y aprendizaje, 66,* 71.

Palsha, S., & Wesley, P. (1998). Improving quality in early childhood environments through on-site consultation. *Topics in Early Childhood Special Education, 18*(4), 243–253.

Peisner-Feinberg, E. S., & Burchinal, M. R. (1997). Relations between preschool children's child care experiences and concurrent development: The cost, quality, and outcomes study. *Merrill-Palmer Quarterly, 43,* 451–477.

*Peisner-Feinberg, E. S., Burchinal, M. R., Clifford, R. M., Culkin, M. L., Howes, C., Kagan, S. L., . . . & Zelazo, J. (1999). The children of the Cost, Quality and Child Outcomes in Child Care Centers Study go to school: Technical Report. Frank Porter Graham Child Development Center, University of North Carolina at Chapel Hill.

*Peisner-Feinberg, E. S., Burchinal, M. R., Clifford R. M., Culkin, M. L., Howes, C., Kagan, S. L., & Yazejian, N. (2001). The relation of preschool child-care quality to children's cognitive and social developmental trajectories through second grade. *Child Development, 72*(5), 1534–1553.

*Peisner-Feinberg, E. S. (2017). North Carolina Pre-Kindergarten Program evaluation: Key findings (2002–2016). Frank Porter Graham Child Development Institute, University of North Carolina.

*Perlman, M., Zellman, G. Z., & Le, V. (2004). Examining the psychometric properties of the Early Childhood Environment Rating Scale–Revised (ECERS-R). *Early Childhood Research Quarterly, 19,* 398–412. doi: 10.1016/j .ecresq.2004.07.006

Phillips, D., McCartney, K., & Scarr, S. (1987). Child care quality and children's social development. *Journal of Applied Developmental Psychology, 23,* 537–543.

Phillips, D., Scarr, S., & McCartney, K. (1987). Dimensions and effects of child care quality: The Bermuda study. In D. Phillips (Ed.), *Quality in child care: What does research tell us? NAEYC Monograph Series, Volume 1.* National Association for the Education of Young Children.

*Phillipsen, L. C., Burchinal, M. R., Howes, C., & Cryer, D. (1997). The prediction of process quality from structural features of child care. *Early Childhood Research Quarterly, 12*(3), 281–303.

*Pianta, R., Howes, C., Burchinal, M., Bryant, D., Clifford, R. M., Early, D. M., & Barbarin, O. (2005). Features of pre-kindergarten programs, classrooms,

and teachers: Prediction of observed classroom quality and teacher–child interactions. *Applied Developmental Science, 9*(3), 144–159.

*Pianta, R. C., La Paro, K. M., & Hamre, B. K. (2008). *Classroom assessment scoring system [CLASS] manual: Pre-K.* Brookes.

*Pinto, A. I., Pessanha, M., & Aguiar, C. (2013). Effects of home environment and center-based child care quality on children's language, communication, and literacy outcomes. *Early Childhood Research Quarterly, 28,* 94–101.

*Raju, N. S. (1990). Determining the significance of estimated signed and unsigned areas between two item response functions. *Applied Psychological Measurement, 14*(2), 197–207.

*Resnick, G. (2010). Project Head Start: Quality and links to child outcomes. In A. J. Reynolds, A. J. Rolnick, M. M. Englund, & J. A. Temple (Eds.), *Childhood programs and practices in the first decade of life.* Cambridge University Press.

*Resnick, G., & Zill, N. (2002). *Is Head Start providing high-quality educational services? "Unpacking" classroom processes.* U.S. Department of Health and Human Services. www.acf.hhs.gov/sites/default/files/opre/quality.pdf

*Rijmen, F., Tuerlinckx, F., De Boeck, P., & Kuppens, P. (2003). A nonlinear mixed model framework for item response theory. *Psychological Methods, 8*(2), 185.

*Rivkin, S. G., Hanushek, E. A., & Kain, J. F. (2005). Teachers, schools, and academic achievement. *Econometrica, 73*(2), 417–458.

Roberts, J. E., Burchinal, M. R., Jackson, S. C., Hooper, S. R., Roush, J., Bryant, D., . . . & Zeisel, S. A. (2000). Otitis media in early childhood in relation to preschool language and school readiness skills among Black children. *Pediatrics, 106*(4), 725.

Rossbach, H. G., Clifford, R. M., & Harms, T. (1991). Dimension of learning environments: Cross-national validation of the Early Childhood Environment Rating Scale. Paper presented at the AERA Annual Conference, Chicago.

*Rutter, M. (2002), Nature, nurture, and development: From evangelism through science toward policy and practice. *Child Development, 73,* 1–21. doi: 10.1111/1467-8624.00388

*Ruzek, E., Burchinal, M., Farkas, G., & Duncan, G. J. (2014). The quality of toddler child care and cognitive skills at 24 months: Propensity score analysis results from the ECLS-B. Early *Childhood Research Quarterly, 29,* 12–21. doi: 10.1016/j.ecresq.2013.09.002

*Sabol, T. J., Soliday Hong, S. L, Pianta, R. C., & Burchinal, M. R. (2013). Can rating Pre-K programs predict children's learning? *Science, 341*(6148), 845–846. doi: 10.1126/science.1233517

*Sakai, L. M., Whitebook, M., Wishard, A., & Howes, C. (2003). Evaluating the Early Childhood Environment Rating Scale (ECERS): Assessing differences between the first and revised editions. *Early Childhood Research Quality, 18,* 427–445.

*Salciccioli, J., Crutain Y., Komorowski, M., & Marshall, D. (2016). Sensitivity analysis and model validation. In *Secondary Analysis of Electronic Health Records* (pp. 263–271). Springer, Cham. doi: 10.1007/978-3-319-43742-2_17.

*Saltelli, A., Chan, K., & Scott, M. (2000). *Sensitivity analysis*. Wiley Series in Probability and Statistics. John Wiley & Sons.

*Sammons, P., Elliot, K., Sylva, K., Melhuish, E., Siraj-Blatchford, I., & Taggart, B. (2004). The impact of pre-school on young children's cognitive attainments at entry to reception. *British Educational Research Journal, 30,* 691–712. doi: 10.1080/0141192042000234656

Sammons, P., Sylva, K., Melhuish, E., Siraj-Blatchford, I., Taggart, B., Smees, R., . . . & Sadler, S. (1999). *The effective provision of pre-school education [EPPE] project: Characteristics of the EPPE project sample at entry to study.* Technical paper 2. Institute of Education, University of London, London, England.

Sammons, P., Sylva, K., Melhuish, E., Siraj-Blatchford, I., Taggart, B., & Elliot, K. (2003). Measuring the impact of pre-school on children's cognitive progress over the pre-school period. In K. Sylva (Ed.), *The effective provision of pre-school education (EPPE) project*. Institute of Education.

*Santosa, F., & Symes, W. W. (1986). Linear inversion of band-limited reflection seismograms. *SIAM Journal on Scientific and Statistical Computing, 7*(4), 1307–1330.

Scarr, S., Eisenberg, M., & Deater-Deckard, K. (1994). Measurement of quality in child care centers. *Early Childhood Research Quarterly, 9*(2), 131–152.

*Schilder, D., & Leavell, A. S. (2015). Head Start/child care partnerships: Program characteristics and classroom quality. *Early Childhood Education Journal, 43*(2), 109–117.

*Schmitt, S. A., Geldhof, G. J., Purpura, D. J., Duncan, R., & McClelland, M. M. (2017). Examining the relations between executive function, math, and literacy during the transition to kindergarten: A multi-analytic approach. *Journal of Educational Psychology, 109*(8), 1120–1140. doi: 10.1037/edu0000193

*Setodji, C. M., Le, V. N., & Schaack, D. (2013). Using generalized additive modeling to empirically identify thresholds with the ITERS in relation to toddlers' cognitive development. *Developmental Psychology, 49,* 632–645. doi: 10.1037/a0028738

*Shaffer, D., & Kipp, K. (2010). *Developmental psychology: Childhood and adolescence*, 8th edition. Thomson Wadsworth.

*Shager, H., Schindler, H. S., Magnuson, K., Duncan, G. J., Yoshikawa, H., & Hart, C. (2013). Can research design explain variation in Head Start research results? A meta-analysis of cognitive and achievement outcomes. *Educational Evaluation and Policy Analysis, 35,* 76–95.

Sheridan, S. (1997). *Evaluations of quality with the Early Childhood Environment Rating Scale: A comparison between external evaluations and preschool teachers' self-evaluations of quality with the ECERS*. Gothenburg University, Department of Education.

Sheridan, S., Giota, J., Han, Y., & Kwon, J. (2009). A cross-cultural study of preschool quality in South Korea and Sweden: ECERS evaluations. *Early Childhood Research Quarterly, 24*(2), 142–156

*Sheridan, S., & Schuster, K. (2001). Evaluation of pedagogical quality in early childhood education: A cross-national perspective. *Journal of Research in Childhood Education, 16*(1), 109–125.

Sideris, J., Clifford, R. M., & Neitzel, J. (2014). New scoring options for ECERS-R. Working paper, Frank Porter Graham Child Development Institute, University of North Carolina at Chapel Hill.

*Smith, M. W., Dickinson, D. K., Sangeorge, A., & Anastasopoulos, L. (2002). *User's guide to the Early Language & Literacy Classroom Observation toolkit: Research edition*. Brookes.

*Snyder, T. D., de Brey, C., & Dillow, S. A. (2018). Digest of education statistics 2016 (NCES 2017-094). National Center for Education Statistics, Institute of Education Sciences, U.S. Department of Education, Washington, DC.

*Soukakou E. P. (2012). Measuring quality in inclusive preschool classrooms: Development and validation of the Inclusive Classroom Profile (ICP). *Early Childhood Research Quarterly, 27*(3), 478–488.

Sticksel, S. A. (1999). Preschool quality and classroom variables: Are teacher-to-child ratio, group size, and ethnic diversity predictive of quality? *Dissertation Abstracts International, 60*(4B), 1889.

*Sylva, K., Melhuish, E., Sammons, P., Siraj-Blatchford, I., & Taggart, B. (2004). *The Effective Provision of Pre-School Education (EPPE) Project: Final report: A longitudinal study funded by the DfES 1997–2004*. Institute of Education, University of London/Department for Education and Skills/Sure Start.

Sylva, K., Sammons, P., Melhuish, E., Siraj-Blatchford, I., & Taggart, B. (1999). *The Effective Provision of Pre-School Education [EPPE] Project: An introduction to the EPPE project*. Technical paper 1. Institute of Education, University of London, London, England.

Sylva, K., Siraj-Blatchford, I., Melhuish, E., Sammons, P., Taggart, B., Evans, E., . . . & Sadler, S. (1999). *The effective provision of pre-school education [EPPE] project: Characteristics of the Centres in the EPPE Sample: Observational Profiles*. Technical paper 6. University of London, Institute of Education, London, England.

Sylva, K., Siraj-Blatchford, I., Taggart, B., & Colman, P. (1998). *The Early Childhood Environment Rating Scale: 4 curricular subscales*. Institute of Education, University of London, London, England.

Sylva, K., Siraj-Blatchford, I., Taggart, B., Sammons, P., Melhuish, E., Elliot, K., & Totsika, V. (2006). Capturing quality in early childhood through environmental rating scales. *Early Childhood Research Quarterly, 21*, 76–92. doi: 10.1016/j.ecresq.2006.01.003

*Sylva, K., Siraj, I., & Taggart, B. (2010). *The four curricular subscales extension to the Early Childhood Environment Rating Scale (ECERS-R) with planning notes*, 4th edition. Teachers College Press.

*Thissen, D., Steinberg, L., & Wainer, H. (1993). Detection of differential item functioning using the parameters of item response models. In P. W. Holland & H. Wainer (Eds.), *Differential item functioning* (pp. 67–113). Lawrence Erlbaum.

*Thurstone, L. L. (1947). *Multiple-factor analysis: A development and expansion of the vectors of mind*. University of Chicago Press.

*Tibshirani, R. (1996). Regression shrinkage and selection via the lasso. *Journal of the Royal Statistical Society: Series B (Methodological), 58*(1), 267–288.

Tietze, W., Bairrao, J., Leal, T. B., & Rossbach, H. G. (1998). Assessing quality characteristics of center-based early childhood environments in Germany and Portugal: A cross-national study. *European Journal of Psychology of Education, 13*(2), 283–298.

*Tietze, W., Cryer, D., Bairrao, J., Palacios, J., & Wetzel, G. (1996). Comparisons of observed process quality in early child care and education programs in five countries. *Early Childhood Research Quarterly, 11*(4), 447–475.

*Tutz, G. (1990). Sequential item response models with an ordered response. *British Journal of Mathematical and Statistical Psychology, 43*(1), 39–55.

*U.S. Department of Health and Human Services. (2017). *Head Start program performance standards*. Head Start Early Childhood Learning and Knowledge Center. https://eclkc.ohs.acf.hhs.gov/sites/default/files/pdf/hspps-final .pdf

*Vermeer, H. J., IJzendoorn, M. H., Cárcamo, R. A., & Harrison, L. J. (2016). Quality of child care using the environment rating scales: A meta-analysis of international studies. *International Journal of Early Childhood, 48*, 33–60. doi: 10.1007/s13158-015-0154-9

Votruba-Drzal, E., Coley, R. L., & Chase-Lansdale, P. L. (2004). Child care and low-income children's development: Direct and moderated effects. *Child Development, 75*(1), 296–312.

*Vygotsky, L. S. (1978). *Mind in society: The development of higher psychological processes*. Harvard University Press.

*Watkins, M. W. (2018). Exploratory factor analysis: A guide to best practice. *Journal of Black Psychology, 44*(3), 219–246.

*Weiland, C., Ulvestad, K., Sachs, J., & Yoshikawa, H. (2013). Associations between classroom quality and children's vocabulary and executive function skills in an urban public prekindergarten program. *Early Childhood Research Quarterly, 28*, 199–209. doi: 10.1016/j.ecresq.2012.12.002

Wesley, P. (1994). Providing on-site consultation to promote quality in integrated child care programs. *Journal of Early Intervention, 18*(4), 391–402.

*Whitebook, M., Howes, C., & Phillips, D. A. (1989). *Who cares? Child care teachers and the quality of care in America*. The National Child Care Staffing Study, Child Care Employee Project.

White House. (2013). *Early learning.* www.whitehouse.gov/issues/education
    /early-childhood

*World Bank. (2019). *Promoting holistic child development: Opportunities for syn-
    ergistic investments in early years in Nepal.* World Bank, Washington, DC.
    https://openknowledge.worldbank.org/handle/10986/33897

*World Health Organization (WHO). (2016, October 5). *Investing in early child-
    hood development essential to helping more children and communities thrive, new
    Lancet Series finds.* WHO. www.who.int/news/item/05-10-2016-investing
    -in-early-childhood-development-essential-to-helping-more-children
    -and-communities-thrive-new-lancet-series-finds

*Yakshina, A. N., Le-Van, T. N., Zadadaev, S. A., & Shiyan, I. B. (April, 2021).
    Design and approbation of evaluation Scale for the conditions of play
    development in preschool groups. Submitted for Publication.

*Yazejian, N., Bryant, D., & Kennel, P. (2013). Implementation and repli-
    cation of the Educare model of early childhood education. In T. Halle,
    A. Metz, & I. Martinez-Beck (Eds.), *Applying implementation science in early
    childhood programs and systems* (pp. 209–225). Brookes.

Zellman, G. L., & Perlman, M. (2006). Parent involvement in child care set-
    tings: Conceptual and measurement issues. *Early Child Development & Care,
    176*(5), 521–538.

Index

About the Authors

Richard M. Clifford is a senior scientist emeritus at the Frank Porter Graham Child Development Institute, University of North Carolina at Chapel Hill. His PhD is in education from UNC-CH. He has been involved in studying public policies and advising public officials and practitioners on policies affecting young children and their families, with particular emphasis on public financing of programs and the provision of appropriate learning environments. Dr. Clifford has edited several books and journal issues as well as authored numerous published articles. He helped to establish and served as the first director of the Division of Child Development in the NC Department of Human Resources and helped design and implement the NC Smart Start initiative. He was also instrumental in the establishment of North Carolina's pre-kindergarten program. He is a past president of NAEYC.

Noreen Yazejian is a senior research scientist and lead of the Research and Evaluation Division, Frank Porter Graham Child Development Institute, University of North Carolina at Chapel Hill. Dr. Yazejian's early childhood research and program evaluation studies have focused on professional development, models of programming from birth to 5, home visiting, quality rating and improvement systems, early childhood language and literacy, and the use of data for continuous quality improvement. Her research has been published in *Child Development, Early Childhood Research Quarterly, Early Education and Development, Social Policy Report,* and *NHSA Dialog.*

Wonkyung Jang is a PhD candidate at the School of Education, University of North Carolina at Chapel Hill. Jang's research interests lie in investigating linguistic environments of early childhood classrooms and the relation between enhanced language learning and classroom experiences, the effects of teacher- or parent-implemented interventions on children's learning, and innovative statistical and computational techniques that can better capture individual differences in language development among children with diverse developmental, cultural, linguistic, and educational needs. While pursuing his doctorate, he earned an MS in statistics and a graduate certificate in computational linguistics. He also has worked during the past 5 years as a research assistant in the Frank Porter Graham Child Development Institute and the School of Education.

Dari Jigjidsuren, PhD, is a research fellow and a visiting scholar at the Social Science Research Center of the Mississippi State University. Dari's research experience is mainly focused on interventions to ensure early childhood well-being, with an emphasis on marginalized children. Through her work at the Frank Porter Graham Child Development Institute in Chapel Hill, Dari participated in the evaluation of Part C program services in Arkansas; collected and analyzed data on child and teacher outcomes for the North Carolina state school system, including the project to promote social emotional foundations for early learning; and provided support to the team working to revise DEC Recommended Practices. From 2016 through 2019 Dari lived in Mongolia, where she conducted research including the baseline study on domestic violence among young children, established a nonprofit to advocate for patients with rare diseases, and served as an advisor to the Mongolian disability portal "We Can Do MN." She also continued working on the data analysis for the validation of the ECERS-3 and ITERS-3. Upon her return to the United States in 2019, Dari has completed her work on the ECERS-3 guide and continues being involved in education research at MSU.